Reading and Writing for Success

Lynn Archer

Cathy Costello

Debbie Harvey

Contributing Authors:

David Friend Christel Kleitsch

HARCOURT
BRACE
CANADA

Canadian Cataloguing in Publication Data

Archer, Lynn
Reading and writing for success

ISBN 0-7747-0197-8

1. Readers (Secondary). 2. English language. I. Harvey, Debbie, 1952– . II. Costello, Cathy. III. Title.

PE1408.A72 1997   808'.0427   C97-932148-4

THE AUTHORS

Lynn Archer is a Vice-Principal at Burnaby South Secondary School in Burnaby, British Columbia, who works with teachers to enhance language and literacy learning. Lynn has developed numerous resources for teachers to use in the classrooms and is very involved in promoting the integration of assessment and evaluation with instruction. A presenter at many educational conferences and seminars, Lynn brings a wealth of expertise to the development of this resource.

Cathy Costello is the English Consultant for York Region Board of Education in Ontario. She spends much of her time assisting teachers to ensure their students achieve literacy outcomes in the classroom. Cathy is an active member of the Secondary School Teachers Federation and is a frequent presenter at conferences.

Debbie Harvey is English department head and a Senior High English teacher at Central Kings Rural High School in Cambridge Station, Nova Scotia. Deb frequently gives seminars on critical literacy for the Nova Scotia Department of Education and Culture.

The Contributing Authors

David Friend is a writer, editor, and teacher who has contributed to the development of a wide variety of educational resources, especially for high school English.

Christel Kleitsch is an author, editor, and former teacher who writes for a wide variety of educational and trade publications.

REVIEWERS

Judy Ballah
English Department Head
Halifax West High School
Halifax, Nova Scotia

Sue Harper
English Department Head
John Fraser Secondary School
Mississauga, Ontario

Maggie Kortes
former English teacher
Old Scona Academic High School
Edmonton, Alberta

Ken Roy
English Department Head
Lakeshore Collegiate
Etobicoke, Ontario

A very special thank you to Maggie Kortes and Ken Roy who gave many hours of their time supporting this project from its inception to its completion. Thank you also to David Bertram, a teacher at Baythorn Public School, Ontario, and his grade eight class, for field testing the Repair Manual for the Top 10 Grammar Errors.

Project Manager: Lydia Fletcher
Supervisiong Editor: Donna Adams
Manager of Editorial Services: Nicola Balfour
Senior Production Editor: Margot Miller
Production Manager: Gaynor Fitzpatrick

Production Assistant: Donna Dowsett
Manager of Art and Design: Dennis Boyes
Text and Cover Design, Art Direction, and
Page Composition: Sharon Foster Design
Permissions Editor: Mary Rose MacLachlan

Cover Illustration
Expressing freedom of imagination, and a striving for enlightenment and achievement, the elements within the illustration show the means by which students will attain skills and knowledge on route to becoming successful readers and writers.

 Printed in Canada on acid-free paper

2 3 4 5 01 00 99

Table of Contents

WHAT DO GOOD WRITERS DO?

Writing About Ideas and Information

Writing Power Tools

There are seven different icons in this book that draw your attention to special features.

Points you to text references.

Invites you to complete an activity.

Invites you to respond to questions/comments about the reading selection.

Oral and Visual Communication Power Tools . . 230

Identifies places where computer programs and the Internet will make your task easier.

Explains the features of the genre.

Defines the specific reading genre or type of writing.

Offers suggestions for enjoying the genre.

What Do Good Readers Do?

You read for many different reasons. You read for entertainment, for information, and to learn. Sometimes reading is fun, but sometimes it's hard work. Reading is an active process. Think of it as a conversation between you—your thoughts, questions, and experiences—and the words on the page.

Below are the four stages in the reading process, with some suggested activities for each stage. You can decide which activities would be most helpful for each reading task you undertake.

1. Before Reading

The first step is to get to know the selection you are going to read. Look it over and use some of the following strategies to get an idea of what it is like.

- Make predictions based on the title, the name of the author, and any other words or illustrations on the cover.
- Read any headings, subheadings, and captions.
- Ask questions about the topic.
- Examine any maps, photographs, graphs, charts, tables, illustrations, and pictures.
- Skim the table of contents and select the chapters or sections you find most interesting or useful.
- Recall what you already know about the subject or content.

2. Reading

Now that you know something about the selection, dive in and read through it. As you read, think about your own responses to the material using some of these strategies.

- Just read and enjoy.
- Keep a Reading Response Journal.
- Think about or take notes on what you've read.
- Ask questions about anything you don't understand or don't agree with.
- List words you don't know and look them up in a dictionary.
- Discuss your responses to the selection with other readers.
- Make connections to what you know already or have read elsewhere.
- Pay attention to any pictures or images that you think of as you read.

3. Rereading

This is your chance to get more out of what you have read: to clarify your understanding of it and to gather information for class assignments. At this stage, you might

- Read the selection aloud, either to yourself or to others.
- Review the selection again to fill in gaps in your notes.
- Create webs, charts, graphs, and other diagrams to organize information.
- Discuss questions about the selection with a partner.

4. After Reading

This is the time for you to reflect on what you've read, to show your understanding of it, and to use the information in a creative way. You might

- Make a follow-up entry in your Response Journal.
- Prepare a Reader's Theatre presentation of part or all of the selection.
- Have a debate on the main topic of the selection.
- Write an essay or prepare an oral presentation about the selection, or use information from the selection in an essay or report.
- Answer any questions or do any activities included within the selection.
- Discuss the selection with another reader.
- Review any notes you made while reading and revise them where necessary.

Different Selections, Different Approaches to Reading

The reading process is not a set of rules; it is a set of possibilities. You don't follow the same steps in the same order every time you read. You may read the same selection in different ways, depending on your reason for reading it. For example, if you read a novel for your own enjoyment, you may read it very quickly. But if you have to write an essay about the novel, you may read it more slowly and carefully. Look at the suggested reading process for each of the following reading tasks.

Reading a Novel for pleasure

Before Reading	**Reading**	**Rereading**	**After Reading**
Choose a novel.	Read quickly and enjoy.		Tell a friend about it.

Reading a Textbook Chapter to prepare for a test

Before Reading	**Reading**	**Rereading**	**After Reading**
Skim the chapter and ask questions.	Read slowly. Take notes and ask questions.	Fill in gaps in notes. Create a diagram.	Answer questions.
			Review notes and answers to questions.

Reading a Poem to prepare for class discussion

Before Reading	**Reading**	**Rereading**	**After Reading**
Make predictions.	Read slowly and enjoy.	Read poem aloud.	Discuss with another reader.
			Reread and create a diagram or illustration.
			Write an entry in your Response Journal.

Reading for Appreciation and Enjoyment

When you read a story, you may interpret it differently at different times, based on the details of the story, how you are feeling, and your life experiences. Your interpretation will affect how much you enjoy the story. The same is true for your appreciation of poetry and drama.

This unit offers strategies you can use to help you understand, interpret, and appreciate short stories, poetry, and drama. The better you understand them, the more you will enjoy reading them, even if you would have told the story differently!

Reading Short Stories

LEARNING EXPECTATIONS
In this section, you will learn
- what the elements of a short story are
- how to summarize the elements of a short story
- how to use a Response Journal while reading a story
- how to make a character web

What Is a Short Story?

A short story is a brief tale written to entertain you and keep you turning the pages to find out how it ends. Reading a short story is like taking a trip to a new place inhabited by people you have never met. Short-story authors write to tell you their ideas about people and the world. By sharing the lives of fictional characters, you gain insights into human nature and behaviour. You may also learn something about yourself.

The Elements of a Short Story

A short-story writer quickly pulls you into the lives of the characters and makes you care about their feelings, their relationships, and their problems. Every detail and event in a short story is carefully chosen by the writer to contribute to the overall effect. Here are some of the elements used in writing a short story.

Characters Believable, interesting characters that you care about are at the heart of a good short story. Be alert to how the main characters grow and change through the events in the story.

Setting The setting is the time and place in which the story takes place. The setting often tells you something about the characters and helps to create the atmosphere or mood.

Conflict Challenges, conflict, or struggle are the basis of every story. Characters may struggle with other people, with animals, with the forces of nature, or with something inside themselves.

Point of View Every story is told from a particular point of view. It may be told from the point of view of one character in the story, or from the point of view of a narrator who knows and sees everything.

Plot The plot is the chain of events in a story. Many stories follow a pattern: the author first establishes the characters, the setting, and the conflict, and then adds complications. The climax is the turning point of the story, where the conflict is resolved and the loose ends are tied up.

Suspense Suspense is what makes you worry about the characters and what will become of them. A life-threatening situation, for example, makes for a suspenseful story.

Theme The theme is the main idea in a story. It is what the story has to say about life and human nature. Keep in mind that different readers may interpret the same story in quite different ways.

How to Read a Short Story

Here are some strategies you can use to get the most from reading a short story.

1. Ease into the story. Before you begin to read a story, take some time to get ready.
- Read the title and think about what might happen in the story.
- Do you know this author? If so, what kind of story might this be?
- Look at any illustrations. What do they tell you about the story?
- Read the first page of the story and pause. What do you know so far about the characters, setting, conflict, and point of view? Where do you think the story is going?

2. Get involved in the story. The key to being a good reader is being an active reader. Here are some of the things you can do to be an active reader.
- Ask questions about what is happening.
- Make predictions about what might happen next.

- Put yourself in the characters' shoes.
- Form opinions about what is going on.
- Think about your responses to what you are reading.
- Picture the setting and events in your mind, or even draw them!
- Write down your favourite quotations from the story.
- Make connections to what you already know.

3. Write about the story. Making notes can help you focus your thinking as you read. Here are some ways of writing about a story.
- Use your Response Journal to record your thoughts about the story. (See page 112.)
- Take notes or draw webs to keep track of the characters and events in a complex story.
- Sketch the setting of the story, or draw a map.

Choose two or three of these strategies to help you read the story that follows. You may wish to keep your own notes as you read. The first time you read the story, ignore the notes in the margins. These notes show one person's responses to the story. Then reread the story, this time including the margin notes. When you have read the story for the second time, work through the Tutorials on pages 25 and 27.

THE VISITOR ①

~ ~ ~

Christine Pinsent-Johnson

I was getting fed up with saying goodbye. One month five kids disappeared from my shrinking class at Copelin High School. At this rate, there would be a class of one graduating next year, and that one would be me. ②

I was witnessing the slow death of a town and there was nothing I or anyone else could do about it. All over the world people ③ unite to fight for something they believe in, like preserving an old-growth forest or protecting the ozone. But no one bothered to fight for Copelin. My dad claimed people had simply accepted their fate; they knew the mines wouldn't last forever and now they realized it was time to move on. ④

Last night I overheard my parents talking about moving to St. John's or the mainland. At least my mom was talking; Dad was trying to avoid the discussion.

"The Greenes are leaving next month," Mom said casually while stirring the spaghetti sauce. "Frank got a job in Grand Falls at the mill."

I knew Mom wanted to leave as much as I did. The fridge was cluttered with want ads from the St. John's, Halifax, and Toronto newspapers.

"I guess we'll have to find someone else to play cards with," ⑤ Dad said. His attempt to avoid the discussion.

"That's not the point. We're losing two more good friends." Mom stopped stirring and started rubbing her neck, which stiffened whenever she was upset. "This is really getting ridiculous," she said quietly. "Why don't you start looking . . ."

"We've already been through this, Joanne. I won't be able to find anything better than what I have."

Dad was sitting across the table from me. I kept staring at my biology textbook, hoping they would keep me out of it.

"I'm committed to stay here at least another couple of years," Dad said as he walked over to Mom. He gently placed her hands at her side and began massaging her neck. "You know I wouldn't be able to find anything better."

Dad was one of the last people to work for the Copelin Mining and Refining Company, which had built the town over sixty years ago. He was the property manager for all the residential buildings, and spent his days running after people for overdue rent and closing up empty houses. About once every couple of months he actually sold a house. Usually it was to one of the retired miners and his wife, determined to stay here until they died.

But most of his days were spent knocking on doors, trying to convince unemployed miners and millworkers to pay months of back rent. Last winter he had to change the locks on two families, forcing them out of their homes. One family quickly left Copelin **6** but the other ended up living with their relatives in the trailer park near the highway. They still won't talk to my dad. He never changed any more locks after that.

6 I wouldn't want to have his job!

I had to leave. I couldn't stand another non-discussion about leaving Copelin.

"Where are you going?" Mom asked, when she saw me get up from the kitchen table. "Supper will be ready in half an hour."

"I'm going out. I'll be back in a few minutes."

"Do you think it's a good idea to go out just before supper?" Dad asked, clearing his throat nervously.

Why can't he just say "Don't go out" or "Be back before supper," I thought. "I won't be long," I said, closing the textbook.

"Well, William, you said that the other day. Heh hemmm. And you were late for supper." I hated it when he used my full name. It sounded so fake. As if he was trying too hard. **7**

7 The son doesn't get on well with his dad.

"I'll be back before supper," I snapped, getting even more irritated. I could feel the sweat beading on my forehead in the steamy kitchen. The window beside the stove was dripping with condensation. I had to get out of there.

"Don't use that tone with your father," said Mom sharply.

Why does she have to stick up for him? Why can't he just say I'm being a brat and get it over with? I couldn't even look at him. I kept staring at the moisture droplets racing down the window.

"As long as you say you'll be back, I guess you can go."

"Gee, thanks Dad." I knew I was being a jerk but I couldn't help it.

As I grabbed my coat off the living room chair I heard Mom say, "You know, you really shouldn't let him talk to you like that." Unbelievable.

The night air was overwhelmed by the sharp, almost suffocating smell of pine smoke from people's wood stoves. It had been raining the past few days, and there was a hazy mixture of fog and wood smoke hanging over the town.

Most of the snow had washed away except for some skeletal remains along the edges of the street and in the ditches. Everyone kept saying they were lucky it was such a mild winter because there was no money for snowplowing. But now the potholes needed to be filled, and there was no money for that either.

Out of a dozen homes on the street five were empty. At the Purdys' house the front door was wide open, leaving the house exposed. I could look straight into the empty living room, where Mrs. Purdy used to sit and wait for her daughter, Michelle, after I walked her home from the dances at the stadium last summer. I ran up the front steps and quickly shut the door.

I turned onto Main Street, walked past the empty lot where the theatre used to be. It had burnt down along with the bowling alley and company store ten years ago. The company only rebuilt the store. They'd stopped showing movies at the theatre anyway, **8** and said it was too expensive to rebuild the bowling alley. The only thing left besides the company store was the bank, post office, and Reid's Bakery, which didn't sell sweets any more, just bread and rolls.

Four streets ran perpendicular to Main. Three of these streets **9** were filled with row houses, three units to a row, three bedrooms in a home. They were neat, orderly army-style homes, low on looks and high on efficiency. No grass in the yards, only rocks and weeds. Almost every home had a clothesline, cutting across the back yard, supported by a cedar rail in the middle. The fourth street, which was ours, was a combination of row homes and small single houses that looked just like row houses, except for the metre gap in between. The bigger single homes were uptown, closer to the mine offices. They were for the geologists, engineers, and office employees. The miners with families lived downtown, and the

8 I can almost see the town. What a sad place!

9 This is a small town!

men from around the bay lived in the bunk houses on the outskirts of town.

I should have been born twenty years ago when the mines were still running and the company took care of everything. There was 10 no other place like Copelin in all of Newfoundland. For a small town, about 3,000 at its peak, Copelin had everything you'd find in a city like St. John's or Corner Brook. There was a movie theatre, restaurant, bowling alley, shooting range, swimming pool, playing fields, and a stadium. For years, Copelin had one of the best hockey teams on the island. The company would even pay for train tickets so fans could cheer on the team during road games. Now there wasn't even a hockey team. It wasn't fair.

≈ ≈ ≈

In early spring Spruce first wandered into town. He was seen **11** ambling silently down Main Street, stooping occasionally to munch the dandelions growing beside the road, as if he were doing nothing out of the ordinary. Mrs. Tilley saw him first, although she **12** didn't know what she saw at the time. I heard her in the post office talking to a group of women.

"My dears, you're not going to believe what I saw last night," she said breathlessly. "I was out for my walk and when I rounded the corner of Ore Street I stared straight into the glaring red eyes of the devil itself."

The women in the post office passed knowing glances to each other and smiled politely. Mrs. Tilley was known for spending long nights at the union hall and staggering home just before her husband woke up.

"You must have been frightened," said the postmaster, from behind the counter.

Mrs. Tilley didn't seem to notice his mocking tone. "My dears, I nearly jumped out of me skin. Them eyes was some creepy, and he didn't even move. I just backed up slow so I wouldn't startle him. Then I high-tailed it home."

At first everyone thought Mrs. Tilley had had one too many until Reverend Sharpe saw Spruce a couple of days later. The devil which appeared in front of Mrs. Tilley was actually a young bull moose. This time, he was spotted downtown, sniffing around the **13** trash bins behind the company store.

10 I can understand his feelings.

11 This is a new part of the story.

12 Who or what is Spruce? An animal of some kind.

13 Oh, Spruce is a moose.

Then later that same morning, Daisy Miller said she saw Spruce in the empty lot beside the bank, where the theatre once stood. He was again nuzzling through the trash cans.

After the first sightings people began to see Spruce a couple of **14** times a week. It was Daisy Miller who started calling him Spruce. Ten years ago her Uncle Spruce and a few other men rescued a moose that had fallen through the ice up on Beothuk Lake. It was Spruce Miller who crawled across the ice to lasso the semi-conscious moose, which they tied to a bulldozer from one of the mines, and hauled out.

I first saw Spruce a few days later. He began to get a little bolder and wandered into town during the late afternoons. He usually came out of the bush at the north end of town around three o'clock, as if he was waiting for a polite time to come calling.

I was struggling with the last question on a math test. Looking out the classroom window for some divine inspiration, I saw Spruce strolling through the school yard. I watched him in silence, hoping no one else would notice him. There were only five other students in my grade ten class. Ever since I was in grade six the school board had been threatening to close the school and bus everyone into the nearest town, an hour's drive up the highway.

Spruce was taking his time, obviously having no destination in mind. He was a picture of contradictions. His long spindly legs looked like they would break under his round bulk of a body. His soft brown eyes were overwhelmed by a massive snout which ended with a flapping upper lip, and his ears looked too small for his long, narrow face. His antlers were just beginning to grow and were covered with a velvety soft fuzz. I was surprised to see how gracefully he moved. I always thought moose were awkward-looking and clumsy, with their long, homely faces and humped backs.

I'd seen a couple of moose before, slung over the hood of a car after being hit on the highway or in the back of a pickup after hunting. My father was probably the only man in Copelin who didn't hunt, so I'd never seen a moose in the wild.

Just that morning, I'd overheard Albert Smith talking to Amanda Higgins, the bank teller, about the moose's lack of intelligence.

"He must be some stunned to come wandering into a town full of hunters," said Mr. Smith on the steps of the company store. "Don't he realize people here live all winter on a freezer full of his distant relatives?"

Amanda Higgins' double chin shook in agreement, "Maybe he's one of them backward moose. Maybe he's brain-injured."

"He'll be brain-injured if he don't quit eating my flowers. Sure, last week I found all my tulips stripped bare. I woulda' got my shotgun and killed him right then and there if I'd caught him."

Amanda Higgins' chins jiggled with excitement. They looked like the dewlap under Spruce's chin. "Yes bye. I knows I'd be hollerin' after him if I caught him in my garden. The animal's got no sense. No sense at all."

But not everyone thought Spruce was a nuisance. People began to set out treats for him, including my father. Rumour was he ate all the Purity Lemon Creams but left the carrots. Every time a sighting was made, Dad would run into the kitchen, grab a handful of biscuits and a couple of apples and set them on the back porch. One night I heard him walking around the back yard just after 2 a.m. He was calling out to the night, "Come on Spruce my son. I've got your favourites here."

I don't know if Spruce ever came that night. Dad was still out there when I fell asleep and neither of us said anything the next morning.

≈ ≈ ≈

When I walked in the door after playing road hockey in front of Dave Rideout's place, the first thing I heard was the booming

---

15 I've never seen a moose this close.

16 I hope nobody shoots Spruce!

17 I didn't know that wobbly part is called a dewlap.

18 Funny—a moose eating cookies.

19 New part of the story.

voice of Reverend Sharpe. He and Dave's father were having a cup of coffee with Dad in the kitchen. The two of them were on the town council; Mr. Rideout was the mayor and the Reverend was a councillor.

"He's getting to be a nuisance," said Reverend Sharpe. "Last week he dug up three flower gardens, eating up people's hard work and enjoyment."

"I heard he's been dragging people's trash all over their yards," said the mayor. "What happens if he ever gets aggressive and goes after one of the kids? You know kids. A little harmless teasing and in a second they could have a two-ton moose chasing after them."

"Sure, I heard Fanny Reid nearly ran into him as she rounded the corner of Main Street in her car the other evening. There he was standing in the middle of the road, refusing to budge," said the Reverend.

"It's our responsibility to do something before someone gets hurt," added the mayor. He was looking straight at my father, waiting for his input. The mayor often stopped by to discuss council issues with my dad. I guess my dad had a certain status in the town as one of the last company employees. Dad also gave the mayor an ego boost, since he would never disagree with him. **20**

My father remained silent. I could see him swallowing, his Adam's apple bulging, as he prepared to clear his throat. But he didn't say anything. He didn't always agree with everything the mayor and Reverend did on council, like the decision to stop subsidizing the summer baseball league, but he went along with them anyway.

Come on, say something, I silently urged from the hall. I knew he disagreed with them. He'd set out at least two bags of apples and three packages of biscuits since Spruce started visiting regularly. I could feel myself turn red when I heard him clear his throat. I slowly backed down the hall and went upstairs to my room.

≈ ≈ ≈

The mayor called a town meeting to discuss Spruce. Once people found out that the mayor was thinking about getting rid of the moose they began to take sides. It was all they could talk about for a week. Petitions were sent around and signs were posted in front yards and along fences, some saying Let Him Be and others saying

20 Uh-oh. His dad always goes along with the mayor.

He's Got To Go. I'd never seen people get so worked up over something. No one protested this much when the mines closed. **21**

The council meeting was moved from the municipal office, a small room in the basement of the library, to the union hall so everyone could attend. There was a reporter from the St. John's newspaper, which never before bothered with small town council meetings. The reporter wasn't much older than me. He didn't even try to hide his boredom, just yawned and doodled in his steno book.

The moose issue was shuffled to the bottom of the evening's agenda. I think the mayor hoped people would get bored and leave the meeting before it ended. His nerves were frazzled, speaking in front of so many people, and he kept shuffling the papers in front of him. He'd never seen so many bodies at a council meeting. The only people who usually attended the meetings were a couple of old-timers with nothing better to do and the editor of the town paper.

My father asked me to go to the meeting with him. He said it was an important issue for the town, and it went beyond a simple decision to let Spruce stay or to force him out. I agreed to go partly because I was feeling guilty for the way I had been treating him the past few weeks.

After passing motions to recruit another volunteer firefighter, start collecting a dog tax, and approve a letter requesting the donation of library books, they finally reached the end of the agenda. A group of men, followed by a haze of their own cigarette smoke, stepped into the stifling hall, and everyone else stopped shuffling and whispering.

The discussion about Spruce started off respectfully enough. Representatives from both sides of the issue carefully stated their case as we sat in silence. My father looked over at me once, and **22** started to smile but changed his mind and looked down at a piece of folded up paper he was holding.

The mayor, in an attempt at a compromise, asked the audience, "Why don't we get one of them tranquillizer guns, knock him out and let him go somewhere one hundred kilometres from here?"

A man in the back stood up. I'd seen him before, standing outside the Legion every afternoon, waiting for it to open. "We're some stunned to be sitting here arguing about this moose. Why don't we just kill it and get a nice bunch of steaks out of him."

21 How will the people solve the problem of the moose? Why can't they just let him hang around?

22 I'd be on the "let him be" side.

"Yes, bye, we do that and we'll have them peace freaks and animal rights activists accusing us of cruelty to animals," said a woman from the middle of the crowd.

"What harm is he doing to ye. I say we just let him do his thing and leave him alone. It's the proper thing," said Mrs. Tilley. Her husband sat beside her shaking his head.

Then one of the old-timers jumped up and yelled, "Kill him before he tramples some poor child." Someone else in the back yelled, "Let the poor thing alone."

The St. John's reporter jerked his head up and began writing madly. Then everyone got into it. People were yelling back and forth at each other. The mayor kept banging his gavel on the table, but everyone ignored him. The reporter stopped his frantic writing for an instant to take a picture of the mayor yelling at everyone to shut up.

In the middle of the yelling and screaming my father stood up slowly. He never said a word in any sort of public meeting. I wanted to slip into the cracks of the floor and disappear. He unfolded his piece of paper and looked at it quickly. Then he folded it back up

23 Does Willy hope his father will say something, or not?

23

and held it tightly in his hand. The people around us stopped talking and looked at my father. Like a wave, silence gradually fell over the rest of the hall. He just stood there, waiting, gripping on to that piece of paper as if it gave him the strength to stand.

He quietly cleared his throat. His first words didn't quite make it out. Someone yelled, "Speak up, we can't hear you." He stopped. I thought he'd pack it in right there. But he didn't. He looked over at me. I couldn't help it, but I turned my eyes away and stared at my shoes. **24**

24 He doesn't think his father will stand up for Spruce.

He began again, a little louder this time, "Spruce has done something for this town that no one has seen for years."

"Yeah, he's picked up the garbage regularly," some wisecracker yelled out.

"Uh, that's not my point," said Dad quietly. He started to unfold his paper and look at his notes. He was totally thrown off. **25**

25 Is the father ever going to speak his mind?

"Tell them about the treats," I whispered. "Tell them about all the times you and other people set out treats for Spruce, like it was Christmas or something." Dad looked down at me, nodded his head slightly and smiled. Then he released his grip on the paper **26** and let it fall to the floor. I thought he had dropped it and when I bent down to pick it up he whispered, "Leave it there."

26 What were the notes on the paper? Had he planned to say something else?

He began again. This time his voice was loud enough the first time. "How many of us have run into our kitchens to find special treats for Spruce every time he was spotted in town? When is the **27** last time you felt that same excitement about something?"

27 I'm glad he finally spoke up! Good for him!

I looked up at him, hoping he would see that I was listening to every word. **28**

28 Willy's feelings about his father have changed a little.

"Spruce has given us all a little hope, something almost magical, during a time when we don't have much of anything that's good." A few people in front of us were nodding in agreement. "I think it would be a foolish idea to get rid of him. I think we should just let him be." Dad didn't waste any time sitting down. People were still looking at him but he didn't acknowledge their stares.

I could tell people were stunned. No one said a word for a few seconds. The mayor screwed up his face as if he had a bad taste in his mouth. The Reverend shrugged his shoulders and sighed. Once people digested everything an excited buzz spread throughout the union hall. I caught bits and pieces of the conversations around us.

"Maybe he's got a point."

"I can't believe Graham Percy stood up and . . ."

"But what if Spruce . . ."

"I've never heard him say that much at one time."

People were talking as much about my dad as they were about Spruce, but I didn't care. I reached down and picked up the crumpled paper my Dad had dropped and put it in my pocket.

"Thanks for your help, Willy," he said.

"You would have done fine without me. People really listened to what you had to say." I looked straight at him. For the first time I noticed the flecks of gold in his deep brown eyes. I had those same flecks.

"You think so?" He really didn't know. It was like he was a kid looking for someone to say he did the right thing.

"I know so," I said.

$$\approx \quad \approx \quad \approx$$

29 Yay, Spruce!

29 A week later council passed a special by-law protecting Spruce, and he was allowed to wander throughout the town freely. The newspaper article from the St. John's reporter ended up being reprinted in the Globe and Mail. Then early in June a CBC crew from St. John's did a piece about Spruce and troubled times for Copelin. Our forgotten town ended up being on the national news with the help of Spruce!

30 What are the people going to do to keep their town going if there's no work?

30 That summer my dad and a couple of other people, including the mayor, formed the C.C.C., the Citizens' Coalition for Copelin. They helped people get low-interest loans from the government so they could afford to buy their homes. People began painting their houses again, the sidewalks were fixed, and some of the potholes were repaired. Copelin would never be the same as it once was, but

31 It's sort of a happy ending, but there are some loose ends.

31 at least it wouldn't became a forgotten ghost town, and maybe I wouldn't be the only one left by the time I graduated from high school.

Responding to a Story

You will write a critical response to the story "The Visitor."

Understanding the Task

Keeping a Response Journal allows you to keep track of your thoughts about a story, and to see if they change as you think about what you've read. A Response Journal is

- a place where you can record your reactions, thoughts, and opinions about the story, what you think of the characters and events in the story, or how the story relates to your own life.
- a place for making notes on the content and elements of the story and any questions or notes about what happens.
- a place to reflect on *how* the author wrote the story, including the language used, the plot, the characterization, and the point of view. You might ask, "How did this story make me feel? Why do I feel this way?"

Getting Ready

In your Response Journal, you may write about the characters or the plot or the quality of the writing in a story. But it's not enough to say, for example, that a character reminds you of someone you know. You need to support your opinions with details and quotations from the story.

1. **Focusing on the Characters** Put yourself in the shoes of one of the characters. Here are some questions to ask in your Response Journal during and after your reading.
- When was I most involved with what was happening in the story? Why?
- If I could be one of the characters in the story, which would I choose to be? Why?
- How well do I understand why the characters behave the way they do?
- Does anyone in the story remind me of someone I know? If so, who and how?
- Do any of the characters remind me of myself? If so, explain how.

2. **Focusing on the Plot** Here are some ideas to help you keep track of what happened in the story (the plot).

a) You might write questions to yourself as you read. Your questions could be something like these.
- What has happened so far in the story?
- What's going to happen next?
- Is there anything about what happened in the story I don't understand?

After you finish reading, see if you can answer your questions.

b) A second strategy is to make notes as you read the story. Pause after every three or four pages and make notes like these.

- Some important things that have happened so far are….
- A passage that I particularly liked is….
- Three questions I have so far are….
- I think the next thing to happen will be….

3. Focusing on the Writing You can assess the strengths and weaknesses of how the story is written. Here are some questions to consider.

- Did the story keep me interested?
- Which part of the story did I like best?
- Which part of the story did I dislike?
- What questions did the story leave with me?
- What opinions did the author express in this story? Do I agree or disagree?

Writing a Response to a Story

Here is an excerpt from a grade 10 student's response to the novel *Animal Farm*. What does this student's response tell you about the characters, the plot, and the writing of *Animal Farm*?

I understand that this book is supposed to be somewhat of a parody. I also understand that it's supposed to be a story of overcoming oppression in which the animals represent the common man and the farmers are supposed to represent the government. All of this is easy to comprehend. The one thing that frustrates me about this story so far is how unrealistic it is. I mean, no matter how fictitious a story is, it should have some thread of probability to it. How many animals do you know of that can read or write? And how many animals know how to sing songs?

Also, though the book is considered progressive, it still contains the same tired, old stereotypes. One of those stereotypes is that of women. I think George Orwell must have been very sexist. For example, the two prominent female characters in this story are portrayed as ignorant and frivolous….

Veronica Lawrence

Write a Response Journal entry for "The Visitor." Use the following checklist to assess your work. A good response should include at least one of the first five elements in the checklist, and must include the last element.

CHECKLIST: RESPONDING TO A STORY

✓ Did I write about my reactions to the story's characters?

✓ Did I include my thoughts about the events in the story?

✓ Did I make connections between the story and my own life and experiences?

✓ Did I include questions about anything I didn't understand in the story?

✓ Did I comment on the author's writing style?

✓ Did I include details and quotations from the story to support my observations?

Summarizing a Story

LEARNING EXPECTATION
You will learn how to summarize a story.

Understanding the Task

There are many things to think about as you read a short story. Where does the story take place? Who are the main characters and what are the relationships among them? What is the conflict in the story? What are the important events in the plot?

When you reach the end of the story, you may find it helpful to go back over it and prepare a summary. A summary will provide you with ideas for class discussions and for writing tasks based on the story.

Getting Ready

Below are several strategies for summarizing the different elements of a short story. For each story you summarize, choose the strategy that you would find most helpful or appropriate for the story.

1. Relationships Among Characters The characters and how they relate to one another are often the main source of the conflict in a story. In the opening scene of "The Visitor," the writer shows us Willy's family:

who they are, what their concerns are, how they feel about one another, and how they behave toward one another.

One way to summarize what you learn about these characters is to draw a web illustrating the relationships among the characters, as well as their feelings and attitudes. Such a web is called a "sociogram." To draw a sociogram, write down the names of the characters in a story, and then add arrows with labels to show relationships, feelings, beliefs, and attitudes. A two-way arrow shows that something is shared. You can include important animals and things in a sociogram. Below is a partial sociogram summarizing the relationships in Willy's family.

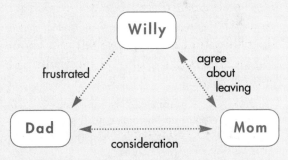

Find examples from the first 10 paragraphs of the story that show each of the feelings and attitudes mentioned in the sociogram. Then draw your own sociogram and add at least three arrows showing other feelings and attitudes related to these three characters. You might look for these other feelings and attitudes in either the kitchen scene (pages 14–16) or the town meeting scene (pages 20–24).

2. Setting In "The Visitor," the setting is a crumbling, half-empty town in Newfoundland. It is one of the main sources of conflict in Willy's family. The setting also reflects Willy's gloomy mood at the beginning of the story.

After the opening scene in the story, Willy goes for a walk through Copelin. You could summarize the setting for that scene on a web or chart like these.

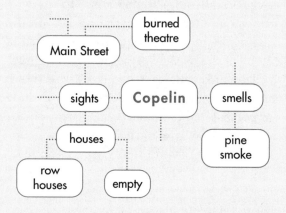

Setting

PLACE:	Copelin, Newfoundland
TIME OF YEAR:	end of winter, early spring
WEATHER:	rainy
THINGS:	row houses
SIGHTS:	skeletal remains of snow
SMELLS:	pine smoke
SOUNDS:	
MOOD:	

Add at least three details to either the web or the chart. Which method would you prefer to use to summarize the setting of a story?

3. Plot Here are two ways to summarize the plot of a story.

a) Cause-and-Effect Chart You can look at the plot of a story as a series of connected events, joined by cause and effect. Something happens, creating an effect. That effect then causes something else to happen, and so on. Look at the following events from "The Visitor." See how they are joined by cause and effect.

Cause	Effect
The mines close down in Copelin.	→ Many people in Copelin lose their jobs. → Many people move away from Copelin.
Spruce comes to Copelin and eats garbage and garden plants.	→ Some people feed Spruce. → Some people talk of killing Spruce.

Notice that each cause can have more than one effect.

Add at least three more cause-and-effect boxes to this chart. Try to show how the effects of the mines' closing and Spruce's arrival relate to each other.

b) Summary Diagram The plot of some stories can also be summarized in a diagram like this.

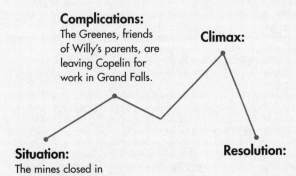

Complications:
The Greenes, friends of Willy's parents, are leaving Copelin for work in Grand Falls.

Climax:

Situation:
The mines closed in Copelin. Many people lost their jobs, but Willy's father is still working and wants to stay. Willy and his mother want to leave.

Resolution:

- The **situation** is the problem or conflict that is introduced at the beginning of the story.
- The **complications** are the main events that lead up to the climax.
- The **climax** is the peak of the action, the most suspenseful moment. In a murder mystery, this might be the moment when the detective reveals the name of the murderer.

- The **resolution** is the part of the story that follows the climax. The tension of the climax relaxes and the author ties up any loose ends. In a murder mystery, this may be where the murderer tells why the murder was committed.

Work with a partner to fill in the rest of this diagram summarizing the events in "The Visitor." Change the shape of the line as needed to fit the number of complications you identify. Before you begin, you and your partner must agree on what the climax of the story is. List the complications in the order they happen in the story. Notice how events cause or lead to other events.

Preparing a Summary

Work with a partner and use one of the ways of summarizing a story described in this Tutorial to summarize the whole story of either "The Visitor" or another story you have read. Make sure that your summary shows how the characters, setting, or plot develops throughout the story. When you have completed your summary, use the checklist below to assess your work.

CHECKLIST: SUMMARIZING A STORY

✔ Did I mention all of the main characters in the story?

✔ Did I describe the setting of the story?

✔ Did I identify the main conflict or challenge in the story?

✔ Did I show the development of the characters, the plot, or the setting throughout the story?

✔ Did I identify the climax of the story?

✔ Is my summary brief and well organized?

Reading Poetry

LEARNING EXPECTATIONS
In this section, you will learn
- how to read a poem
- how to write a response to a poem
- how to recognize the elements of poetry

What Is a Poem?

A poem is a concise verbal snapshot of a poet's thoughts. Poems work through the **images** they paint, the **sounds** they create, and the **ideas** they communicate.

You need to read a poem more than once—and at least one time out loud, so you can hear the sounds and rhythms. Close your eyes and try to see the pictures painted by the words. Try to share the poet's feelings and perceptions. Then ask yourself, "What does this poem say to *me*?"

The Elements of a Poem

Poets combine sounds, images, and shapes to make a unique creation in words that communicate with you, the reader.

The Music of Poetry: Its Sounds Poetry needs to be read aloud. As you read, listen for words that rhyme and for a rhythm you can tap your fingers to, like music. Listen for words that imitate sounds you hear around you in real life. And listen for letter sounds that repeat. All these sounds add to the effect of the poem.

The Images of Poetry: Its Pictures As you read poetry, let the poet's words paint pictures in your mind. Poets use sensory images to appeal to sight, hearing, taste, smell, and touch. Poets often use comparisons that give you new ways of looking at familiar things.

The Structure of Poetry: Its Shape Pay attention to how the poet has placed the words on the page. A new stanza or verse may signal a change of focus or of tone. The poet may repeat lines or words to emphasize important ideas.

How to Read a Poem

Think of reading a poem as having a conversation with the poet. The poet is saying what's on his or her mind and you're listening. But don't just sit there—get involved! Ask questions. Make comments. Express your feelings. Give your opinions. Share your experiences. You can record your side of the conversation in your Response Journal.

Here are some strategies for reading poetry. When you read a poem, choose a strategy that suits the poem and your purpose for reading it.

Getting Ready

Before you start to read a poem, look it over. Find out how long it is, if it is divided into stanzas, or if it has an unusual shape. Read the title and think about what it suggests to you. Scan the poem for words that catch your attention.

Getting to Know the Poem

- Read the poem straight through at least once to get a feel for it. Don't think too much yet about what it means.

- Pay attention to the punctuation as you read. Pause briefly at commas, longer at periods. If there's no punctuation at the end of a line, keep right on reading.

- Listen to the sounds of the words. Read all or part of the poem out loud. Think about what feelings and ideas the sounds suggest.

- Read the poem through slowly, this time thinking about what it means.

- In a dictionary, look up any words that you don't know.

- Try to see in your mind any pictures the poet creates.

Getting Into the Poem

- List things that catch your attention in the poem: repetitions, comparisons, rhymes, images, sounds. Describe the effect they have on you as you read.

- Pick one line that best represents what you think the poem is about.

- Talk about the poem. Share your ideas and questions about the poem.

- Listen to the tone of voice in the poem. It may express an emotion or an attitude. Is it teasing, serious, angry?

- Think about who is speaking in the poem. Some poets write in their own voice, as if they were speaking. Some poets write as another person.

- Look over the notes you have made and read the poem once again. Have any of your first ideas changed? What does the poem mean to you? How does the meaning you found compare to the meanings found by others?

There are two short poems on the following pages. The notes in the margins reflect the thoughts and responses one reader had while reading these poems. Read both poems once, ignoring the margin notes. Make notes of your own, using some of the strategies described above. Then read the poems again, this time including the margin notes. How do your thoughts about the poems compare with those of the reader who wrote the notes? Then work through the Tutorials on pages 34 and 36.

Trombone Solo (1)

I like people (2)
Who strut their stuff;
Any kind of people,
Nice ones or tough.
I like people
With swagger in their step,
Hot-air people, full
Of popcorn and pep, (3)
Four-flushing people (4)
Whose gestures are free —
Strut your stuff, people, (5)
Don't
  mind
    me!

I like people
Who feel their oats (6)
High-stepping people
With ego in their throats,
Telling tall stories,
Taller than the steeple,
Getting away with it —
That kind of people. (7)
If it's done properly,
Carried with an air, (8)
Strut your stuff, people —
I
  won't
    care (9)

— Stoddard King

1 Trombone—sounds like it's about music.

2 Oh, it's about people.

3 This poem rhymes. Nice comparison of people and popcorn.
4 "Four-flushing"? Look it up.
5 Repetition.

6 "Feel their oats/high-stepping"—sounds like horses.

7 Do I like these kinds of people too?

8 What does this mean?

9 This poem is like jazz music.

How does the title relate to the rest of the poem?

Foul Shot (1)

With two 60s stuck on the scoreboard (2)
And two seconds hanging on the clock,
The solemn boy in the centre of eyes,
Squeezed by silence, (3)
Seeks out the line with his feet,
Soothes his hands along his uniform,
Gently drums the ball against the floor,
Then measures the waiting net,
Raises the ball on his right hand,
Balances it with his left,
Calms it with his fingertips, (4)
Breathes,
Crouches,
Waits,
And then through a stretching of stillness, (5)
Nudges it upward.

The ball (6)
Slides up and out,
Lands,
Leans, (7)
Wobbles,
Hesitates,
Exasperates,
Plays it coy (8)
Until every face begs with unsounding screams —

And then,
    And then, (9)
        And then,
Right before ROAR-UP,
Dives down and through. (10)

— Edwin A. Hoey

1 A basketball poem.

2 Tied game; almost over.

3 Lots of "s" sounds.

4 It sounds like the ball is alive, like it's an animal or person.

5 What is a "stretching of stillness"?

6 Why a new verse?

7 Why does he put each verb on a separate line?

8 The ball sounds alive again.

9 Repetition.

10 He made the shot!

Responding to a Poem

Understanding the Task

Every poem that we read creates some kind of reaction in us: "This is a great poem!" "I don't get it." "Boring!" "It's funny."

In a written response to a poem, you move beyond this first reaction to state your thoughts and feelings about the poem more clearly. You try to explain why you feel the way you do about the poem. You must also support your opinion with examples and quotations from the poem.

Getting Ready

One way to better understand your ideas about a poem is to discuss them with a partner. Choose one of the poems on pages 32 and 33 and read it to yourself. Then read it aloud to a partner. Listen to the sound of the words as well as their meaning.

After you've read the poem, write three questions you have about it and discuss your answers with your partner. Here are some questions to get you started.

- How did you feel as you read the poem?
- What was your first response to the poem?
- What are your favourite lines or images?
- What does the poem remind you of from your own experience?
- Which words carried the most meaning?
- Which lines did you find most difficult to understand?

Take time to think about the discussion you've just had.
- Do you both understand the poem better now? Why or why not?
- How did your opinion of the poem change as you talked about it?
- Did you and your partner agree or disagree about the poem? Why?

Preparing a Response

You can use a chart like the one on the next page to prepare a response to a poem.

Work with a partner and use the chart as a model for your own response to "Foul Shot" or another poem of your choice. When you have completed your chart, write a final sentence that describes what you think about the poem overall. Then use the checklist on the next page to assess your work. You may wish to have a classmate read your chart and answer the same questions about it.

Response to Stoddard King's Poem "Trombone Solo"

How did you feel as you read the poem?	I enjoyed the beat, but sometimes had trouble fitting in all the words.
What do you think of the poet's ideas? Do you agree? Why or why not?	I'm not sure whether I agree with them. I don't like people who brag, which is what "With ego in their throats" sounds like. But the way he describes them, they sound kind of fun.
What are your favourite images in the poem? Why did you choose them?	"Hot-air people, full/Of popcorn and pep." I chose this image because I like eating popcorn, and I like people with "pep." All the "p" sounds are sort of fun.
What do you think of the sound of the poem—its rhyme, its rhythm, and the words used?	The beat is good, kind of like rap music, but some of the lines don't quite fit. Especially "Getting away with it." I like the words used to describe people.
How does the poem connect with your personal life?	The title reminded me of the time I played piano at a music festival. I would have enjoyed the festival more if I was like the "high-stepping people" in the poem.
What would you say to the poet about this poem if you had a chance?	I think I would ask him what kind of people he doesn't like, or maybe what he thinks of quiet people.
What do you think the poem is saying?	It's about the kind of people the poet likes.

CHECKLIST: RESPONDING TO A POEM

✓ Did I put the name of the author and the title of the poem at the top of the chart?

✓ Did I answer each of the questions in the chart?

✓ Did I give my own thoughts and feelings about the poem?

✓ Did I use examples from the poem to support my ideas?

✓ Did I make connections between the poem and my own life?

✓ Did I describe in my own words what I think the poem is saying?

Discussing Poetic Language

Understanding the Task

While you read a poem, it is important to remember that every word has been chosen carefully—for its meaning, its sound, its tone, its emotional power, and the picture it paints. The way the poet has arranged the words on the page may also highlight their meaning and importance.

Getting Ready

Poetic language is the same language you use every day. But when poets write, they use fewer words and take far more care about choosing them than you do when you talk to a friend.

You may find examples of poetic language in conversations, stories, news articles, and even textbooks. But you will always find it in poetry. Here are some of the most common characteristics of poetic language.

1. Poetic Imagery Poets use images that appeal to our five senses: to hearing, sight, smell, taste, and touch. Some images may appeal to more than one sense, and not every poem will necessarily have images that appeal to all of the senses. In your Response Journal, connect each of the following images from "Foul Shot" to the sense it appeals to.

hearing	"Seeks out the line with his feet"
sight	"Soothes his hands along his uniform"
smell	"...measures the waiting net"
	"...a stretching of stillness"
taste	"The ball/Slides up and out"
	"Dives down and through"
touch	"Gently drums the ball..."

2. Figures of Speech Poets use the following figures of speech to help us see things in new and unexpected ways.

- **Similes and Metaphors** Poets use similes and metaphors to make comparisons between things that may not seem similar at all. Similes use the words "like" or "as," for example, *The snowflakes were like lace.* Metaphors don't use "like" or "as," for example, *The sun is a flaming torch in the desert sky.*

There are no similes in "Foul Shot" or "Trombone Solo," but there are some metaphors. For example, in "Trombone Solo," the lines "Hot-air people, full/ Of popcorn and pep," compare some people to popcorn, and maybe to hot-air balloons. What other metaphors do you see?

- **Personification** Personification is the description of an object as if it had human qualities or abilities. Look at how the poet makes the ball sound like a person in these lines:

    "Calms it with his fingertips"
    "Plays it coy"

What human qualities do these lines suggest the ball has?

3. Sound Devices Poets use sound devices to help us hear the sounds of certain letters or words.

- **Alliteration** Alliteration is the repetition of a sound made by a consonant. Read the first four lines of "Foul Shot" aloud. Do you hear the "s" sound repeated? What noises at a basketball game might this sound suggest?

- **Onomatopoeia** Onomatopoeia is the use of a word to imitate the sound it names. For example, the word "buzz" sounds just like the noise it names. "Drums" in the first verse of "Foul Shot" and "ROAR-UP" in the last verse are subtler examples of onomatopoeia. What sounds do these words imitate? Can you find other examples of onomatopoeia in either of the poems on pages 32 and 33?

4. Building Mood Right from the opening two lines of "Foul Shot," the poem is full of suspense.

"With two 60s stuck on the scoreboard
And two seconds hanging on the clock"

These describe a tied game with only two seconds left. The foul shot could break the tie and win the game. The poet builds suspense by stretching out the description of the action.

The poet also adds to the suspense by the way he lays out the poem. Here is the second verse of the poem rewritten in three lines:

"The ball slides up and out, lands, leans,
Wobbles, hesitates, exasperates, plays it coy,
Until every face begs with unsounding screams"

Compare the effect of this version with the author's. Which is more suspenseful? Why?

With a partner, find other places where the poet uses the layout of the poem to build suspense. How well do you think this technique works?

5. Vivid Language "Foul Shot" is packed with lively, energetic action words. There are 19 verbs in only 30 lines. The verbs are all in the present tense, making it sound as if the action were happening right now.

Read this version of the first line of the poem.
"With two 60s on the scoreboard"
The line still makes sense, but the effect is far weaker. "Stuck" adds to the sound of the line with the repetition of the hissing "s." "Stuck" also adds to the sense of the line: it suggests that the game is "stuck" in a tie and that the action is temporarily "stuck" as the player prepares to make the shot.

With a partner, identify some of the verbs in "Foul Shot," and discuss how they add to the sound and sense of the poem.

Conducting a Discussion

With a partner, read the poem on the right, "Snow Shadows," and talk about the poetic language used in it. Explain how each example of poetic language you identify adds to the meaning of the poem and its sounds or images. These questions may help you to get started.

- How does the poet describe the way the shadows move?
- What comparisons does he make in the poem?
- Which phrases and lines create the most vivid pictures in your mind?
- How does the poet use repeated sounds? Is it effective?

Before you start your discussion, read the tips for making discussions work well, on page 231. When you've finished your discussion, use the checklist below to assess your experience.

Snow Shadows

Shadows crouch,
cats curled up
asleep
upon the snow.
Comes afternoon
and soon
the cats
with slow
and leisured ease
awake,
bestir,
stretch out their feline length
luxuriously,
then slink
in gliding,
hurrying,
scurrying
flight
to some dark
assignation
in the night.

by Arthur S. Bourinot

CHECKLIST: DISCUSSING POETIC LANGUAGE

✓ Did we discuss how the poem appealed to the senses?

✓ Did we discuss the use of figures of speech?

✓ Did we discuss the mood of the poem?

✓ Did we discuss our thoughts and feelings about the poem?

✓ Did we make connections between the poem and other experiences?

✓ Did we support our ideas with examples and quotations from the poem?

Reading Drama

LEARNING EXPECTATIONS
In this section, you will learn
○ how to recognize the elements of a drama
○ how to read a drama effectively
○ how to perform a dialogue
○ how to better understand characters

What Is a Drama?

A drama is a piece of writing that is meant to be performed by actors for an audience.

A drama uses many of the same elements as a short story—setting, plot, conflict, and character—but uses only the characters' words and actions to tell the story.

Reading a drama is like reading a conversation. You need to follow the action through all the talk.

The Elements of a Drama

Plays, screenplays, teleplays, radio plays, and skits are all dramas. Each is written to be performed in a different setting: on a stage, before a movie or television camera, or on the radio. A skit, or sketch, is a short drama. The written version of any drama is called a script.

Most dramas include some or all of these elements.

The cast of characters lists all the people in the drama. It appears at the beginning of the script and may also include information about the characters. In some plays, the cast of characters is called the "Dramatis Personae."

The setting is the time and place where the action occurs, and it provides the atmosphere or feeling created by the dialogue and images in the play. The atmosphere (or mood) may be happy or sad, terrifying or funny, or a variation of these possibilities.

Stage directions describe the physical set and the actions in a drama—the specific locations and scenery needed, where and how the actors should move, and how they should speak their lines. Most stage directions also describe any special visual images, sound and lighting effects, or music required by the drama.

Acts and scenes are smaller sections within a script. Most plays have two or more acts, and each act is divided into scenes. A new scene or act often signals a break in the action or a change in time or location.

Dialogue is the words spoken by the characters. It reveals the personalities of characters and their relationships with one another.

A monologue is a long speech spoken by one character. It usually says something about that character's thoughts and feelings. Monologues are sometimes called soliloquies. Some dramatists write monologues that are performed by one actor alone on the stage.

How to Read a Drama

When you read a drama, you have to imagine how the words would be spoken and try to see the action in your mind. Reading a drama aloud with a partner or in a group can help improve your understanding and appreciation of it.

Getting Ready

Before you start to read a drama, look over the selection. Find out how long it is and allow yourself enough time to read it through without rushing.

Then read the title, the cast of characters, and the description of the setting and scenery. Try to predict what the drama will be about. Answer these questions.
* Who are the characters and how are they related to each other?
* Where and when does the story take place?
* Does the title suggest any connections to your own life or raise any questions?
* How many acts and scenes does the drama have? Do they have titles?

While You Read

If you are reading a longer drama, keeping notes will help you to follow the story and prepare your response to it. You can pause to make notes between acts or scenes.

The script for one scene from a teleplay is on the following pages. Use some of the strategies described in Getting Ready as you prepare to read it. The first time you read it, try not to look at the notes in the margins. Make notes of your own about the characters, the plot, and your personal responses to the scene. The following questions will help you think about your response.

Characters What are the characters like? What do they want? Do you care about the characters? Why or why not?

Plot What is the source of the conflict or problem in the scene? Is the conflict resolved by the end of it? What is the climax of the scene? Is the ending satisfying?

Personal Response What part of the scene did you like the best? Was there anything about the scene you found confusing? Did the scene say anything interesting about how people behave? If so, do you agree with what it said?

Read the scene again, this time including the notes in the margins. Compare your thoughts with those of the reader who prepared the notes. When you have read the scene a second time, work through the Tutorials on pages 50 and 53.

A Scene From the Teleplay

Ride to the Hill

by Ron Taylor

BACKGROUND

Pauline has grown too big to ride her little pinto, Stanley, so her father has sold him. Pauline has had Stanley for six years and she loves him dearly—she doesn't even want to look at the horse that her father bought to replace him. Stanley is leaving today and Pauline has just finished her last ride with him.

CAST OF CHARACTERS

PAULINE: *a tall, angular fourteen-year-old. She wears jeans, a shirt-like blouse, and riding boots. Her hair is long and straight, at times half covering her face. She is not beautiful, and only at certain moments can she even be called pretty. Her movements are often awkward, but never clumsy.*

MARTIN: *a likable, gregarious, just turned fifteen-year-old. He is stocky in build and short for his age.*

EXTERIOR FIELDS AND CORRAL. DAY. A long shot as Pauline *and the horse approach the lower gate of the corral.*

A figure, sitting on a fence in the corral, leaps down and comes to the lower gate to open it for them. His name is Martin. *As* Pauline *and the horse come through the gate,* Martin *greets them cheerfully.*

MARTIN: Hi!

PAULINE: *(coldly)* Hi.
(Pauline *rides the horse into the corral, slips off his back and ties him to the rail.*)
(Martin *closes the gate and follows them.*)

MARTIN: Well...here I am.
(Pauline *picks up the curry comb and brush and begins working on the horse.*)

PAULINE: He's not ready yet.

MARTIN: He looks fine to me, just as he is.

PAULINE: He's not leaving here until he's groomed. If you don't feel like waiting around, I'll bring him over to your place (1) when I'm finished.

MARTIN: You don't have to do that. I'll wait. *(He watches for a moment.)* Maybe I can help you. (2)

PAULINE: I'd rather do it myself, thank you.
(Martin *nods, climbs onto the fence and sits watching her. After a while of stony silence:*)

MARTIN: Look, I just want you to know, I didn't have anything to do with this. All I know is, your father phoned up my father and before I knew it I had a horse. To tell you the truth, I couldn't care one way or the other. (Pauline *looks up.*) You know, my father's on a great-outdoors kick. He wants to put the whole family on horseback. I wish he'd buy me a (3) motor-bike instead. It's not that I'm afraid of them. Horses, I mean. Is...is this one tame?

PAULINE: You mean gentle?

MARTIN: Yeah. Is he gentle?

PAULINE: No.

MARTIN: *(worried)* Oh. *(Finally he smiles, figuring that she's putting him on.)*

PAULINE: That's because I'm the only one who can come near him.

MARTIN: You're kidding!
(Pauline *steps back.*)

PAULINE: Try him.

---

1 She's being pretty mean to him.

2 He's trying hard to be nice.

3 His father is bossy. Doesn't listen to what Martin wants.

MARTIN: No thanks.
    (Pauline *goes back to grooming the horse.*)
    What...what does he do?

PAULINE: He bites.

4 He doesn't know anything about horses.

MARTIN: You're kidding. A horse? **4**

PAULINE: That's right. He kicks too.
    (Martin *comes down off the fence.*)

MARTIN: Oh for crying out loud!

5 She's kind of overdoing it here. It's not his fault she's losing her horse.

PAULINE: *(laying it on)* And when you try to ride him in the morning, he bucks. **5**
    (Martin *is ready to leave.*)

MARTIN: What the heck did my father buy me a horse like that for?

PAULINE: And one thing I must warn you. Sometimes he rears. He rears right up on his hind legs. He paws the air and rolls his eyes, and snorts through wide-spread nostrils. And once, he tried to fall back on top of me, and crush me with his mighty horse's weight!
    (Martin *has caught on. He looks relieved.*)

6 He tries to see it from her point of view.

MARTIN: You're putting me on. Aren't you? *(As Pauline resumes her work,* Martin *climbs back on the fence.)* I don't blame you. **6** I did the same thing once myself. I used to have an electric train. Automatic switches, cars that uncoupled themselves. You know. The whole bit. I was supposed to give it away to my little cousin because I wan't using it anymore. Only when he came to get it I told him it was dangerous to play with because he might get electrocuted and die, and I held a little piece of metal across the tracks and it made a few sparks and he started crying and yelling and everybody came running, and...anyway he got the train, and I really didn't miss it much. (Pauline *is not impressed.* Martin *shrugs.)* I hear you got a new horse. How do you like him?

PAULINE: I don't know.

MARTIN: Maybe you just have to get used to him. It's the same with me. I'll have to get used to my horse, too. (Pauline *looks up at the strange words "my horse."*) *(pause)* I hear he's very big. Your new one I mean. Seventeen hands? Is that right? It's not seventeen feet is it?

PAULINE: Hardly.

MARTIN: To tell you the truth, I haven't the faintest idea what seventeen hands means. All I know is that it's supposed to be big. How big is this one?

PAULINE: Twelve hands.

MARTIN: Then seventeen hands is...is almost half again as big. Isn't it? Hey, that's not a horse, that's an elephant! (7) *(Pauline looks up coldly.)* What colour is he?

PAULINE: I don't know.

MARTIN: Haven't you seen him yet?

PAULINE: No.

MARTIN: When's he coming?

PAULINE: He's already here.

MARTIN: And you haven't seen him?

PAULINE: No.

MARTIN: Where is he?
  (Pauline turns and looks at the stable.)

PAULINE: In there?

MARTIN: Could I have a look at him?

PAULINE: *(strongly)* No!

MARTIN: O.K. He's your horse.

PAULINE: I don't want anybody looking at him. I don't want anybody stroking him, or saying kind things to him. He's (8) going back. I don't want another horse.

MARTIN: Look. Why don't you keep your horse? This one I mean. Why don't we just forget the whole thing? My father'll phone up your father, and your father can phone the guy who sold him the horse that's seventeen hands—or—feet—or—whatever it is—tall...and you'll have your horse back. *(Martin comes down off the fence.)* What do you say?

PAULINE: *(softening)* I can't.

MARTIN: Sure you can. You want him back, don't you?

PAULINE: Of course.

MARTIN: Then take him. *(Pauline, fighting back the tears, shakes her head.)* Oh for crying out loud! Look, I don't want the

7 Maybe he's trying too hard. Maybe he should just back off and leave her alone.

8 Weird. Why can't someone else be nice to her horse?

horse. I don't even know how to ride one. So would you please do me a favour and take your horse back before I get killed?

PAULINE: *(desperately)* I can't.

MARTIN: Why?
(Pauline is beginning to choke, trying to laugh to keep from crying.)

9 Her father sounds mean.

PAULINE: Because...because my father won't board him **9** anymore. He says I'm making a fool of myself...because I've grown too big for him...and we look so funny together that people...the people...(Martin *is embarrassed. He is also moved, but afraid to show it. Through the choking and tears,* Pauline *senses his embarrassment. She tries her best to stop.)*

10 Hey, she's actually nice to him.

PAULINE: I'm sorry if you have to take a horse that you don't want. **10**

MARTIN: That's alright. I'll just have to learn to ride. That's all.

PAULINE: I could teach you if you like.

11 They're starting to be friends.

MARTIN: Sure, why not? Maybe we could go for rides together. **11** That is if you keep your new horse. (Pauline *turns away and begins to work on the pinto once again.)* Is he really hard to manage? This one I mean. (Pauline *hugs the horse affectionately.)*

PAULINE: He's very gentle and very kind. And he understands everything.

MARTIN: I just hope he understands me.

PAULINE: He will if you give him a chance.

MARTIN: How long have you had him?

PAULINE: Since I was eight.

MARTIN: *(really impressed)* You're kidding!

PAULINE: He knows all about me. All my secrets.

MARTIN: *(This is too much.)* Oh great! What am I doing taking him away from you?

PAULINE: It's not your fault.

MARTIN: Yeah, but why me? I don't even know anything about horses. I don't appreciate that horse.

PAULINE: You will when you get to know him.

MARTIN: I wish my father wouldn't do these things. I feel lousy. I really do.

PAULINE: Please don't. I understand.

MARTIN: I just want you to know that you can come and see him whenever you want.

PAULINE: Thank you.

MARTIN: In fact, I hope you do.

PAULINE: Why?

MARTIN: I don't know...because... *(He shrugs.)* I like you.

PAULINE: Thank you. I like you too.

MARTIN: Who, me? Martin the horse thief?

PAULINE: *(laughing)* You're not a horse thief.

MARTIN: I'm one of the roughest, toughest horse thieves in the country, pardner.

PAULINE: You are not.

MARTIN: Am so.

PAULINE: *(laughing)* You can't even *ride* a horse.

MARTIN: Don't have to. I'm so tough I just pick 'em up and carry 'em away.
(They both laugh, then fall silent, and stand for a moment looking at one another. Finally, a little embarrassed, Pauline resumes working on the horse.)

MARTIN: Do you have a boyfriend?

PAULINE: No.

MARTIN: Great! **12**
(Martin grins. Pauline smiles. Martin begins to take a little walk about the corral, hands in pockets, strutting ever so slightly. He picks up a stone and pitches it out across the corral. He takes another one, and uses a more exaggerated pitching style. He looks at Pauline for approval. Pauline smiles.) **13**

MARTIN: I was a pitcher back home.
(He picks up another stone, takes his stance, checks the imaginary bases, begins a very slow and dramatic windup, and lets fly across the corral. Pauline laughs.)

MARTIN: That's what you call style.

12 This sounds like a romance starting.

13 He's showing off for her. Does he feel insecure about being short?

PAULINE: I'll bet you're good.

MARTIN: Pretty good.
(He comes back and leans against the fence.)

PAULINE: Would you like to help me?

MARTIN: Sure.
(Pauline *hands him the brush and they begin to work together, silently, enjoying each other's company, looking up now and then to meet one another's eyes and to smile. It is a moment in which nothing really needs to be said; nevertheless, after a while,* Martin *is compelled to express himself in words. He steps back from his work.)*

MARTIN: You know, I think I'm going to like it out here in the country. I mean it. You know what I like about it? The space! *(He begins to gesture like someone inspired.)* There's so much space. Fields, and hills, and sky! My gosh, you can actually see the sky. You can smell the air! *(Pauline is enjoying this immensely.)*
You've got so much freedom to be yourself. You don't have to feel that there's a crowd of people looking over your shoulder. It's as if you have all this space, and you're alone in the middle of it, and you can do whatever you like. Look at us. Look at the way we hit it off together. *(Pauline smiles.)*
I think it's terrific! I'll bet if we were in the city we'd never get a chance to know one another. We'd probably be so worried about what people were going to say, or how we'd look (14) walking down the street together that we'd be afraid to stop long enough to talk to each other. Do you know what I mean?

PAULINE: I...I'm not sure.

14 He shouldn't be saying these things to her!

MARTIN: What I mean is...
(*Suddenly he realizes where this is leading. He and* Pauline *face one another, and for a moment neither can speak. Finally:*)

PAULINE: Do you mean that we'd look funny walking down the street together? (Martin *is unable to answer.*) Is that what you mean? Is it because I'm...I'm taller than you are? Is it because I'm so big for my age? Would you be ashamed to be seen with me back home where you come from? Would your friends all laugh at you? Do you think that you don't have to worry about it out here because there's nobody to see us? Is that it?

15

MARTIN: I didn't mean it that way...I...

PAULINE: Yes you did. Only you're wrong. There are people here, too. I know. Maybe there aren't as many, but the ones who are here can hurt you just as much. (*She unhitches the horse.*) Your horse is ready now. You'd better lead him until he gets used to you.
(*For a moment* Martin *hesitates. He is truly ashamed.*)

MARTIN: Look, I...
(Pauline *smiles a gentle, forgiving smile, and hands him the lead.* Martin *begins to take the horse away. He stops and turns.*)

16

MARTIN: I'm an idiot. I really am. I'm such an idiot. What the heck's the matter with me? Why don't I learn to shut up once in a while? I do it all the time!

PAULINE: It's alright. It doesn't matter. (Martin *begins to lead the horse off again.*) Goodbye Stanley.

MARTIN: What?

PAULINE: That's his name, "Stanley."

MARTIN: Gee, what a funny name for a horse. (*He smacks his head.*) You see what I mean!
(*Exasperated, he leads the horse out through the corral gate, and on up the road.* Pauline *watches them go, and as she does, her face begins to lose its composure.*)

PAULINE: (*almost to herself*) Stanley! (*She runs to the gate. Again to herself:*) Goodbye.
(Martin *and the horse are well up the road. After a moment,* Pauline *turns back to the rail. Her P.O.V. [point of view] of the rail. It is empty. She comes forward sadly, picks up the grooming tools and starts to walk to the barn.*) 17

15 Pauline is so sensitive.

16 She doesn't seem to be mad at Martin.

17 Is she going to accept her new horse?

Performing a Dialogue

You will read a dramatic dialogue aloud with understanding.

Understanding the Task

Dramatists reveal characters largely through dialogue. In a realistic, contemporary script like "Ride to the Hill," the words that characters speak should sound natural.

Real conversations are rambling, repetitive, and disorganized. The dialogue in a drama is conversation that has been carefully shaped to tell a story and to entertain an audience.

Getting Ready

Dialogue serves many different functions.

1. It reveals the characters' personalities, thoughts, moods, feelings, opinions, and problems.
2. It shows the relationships among the characters.
3. It moves the plot forward.
4. It creates atmosphere.
5. It gives information about important things that have happened in the past or will happen in the future, and about things that happen during the course of the drama, but not on stage.

Which of the five functions do you think each of the following lines of dialogue serves? Some lines may serve more than one.

*   Pauline: "He's not leaving here until he's groomed." (page 43)
*   Pauline: "I'd rather do it myself, thank you." (page 43)
*   Martin: "Hey, that's not a horse, that's an elephant!" (page 45)
*   Pauline: "Because...because my father won't board him anymore." (page 46)
*   Pauline: "He knows all about me. All my secrets." (page 46)
*   Martin: "I just want you to know that you can come and see him whenever you want." (page 47)
*   Pauline: "Do you mean that we'd look funny walking down the street together?" (page 49)
*   Martin: "Why don't I learn to shut up once in a while? I do it all the time!" (page 49)

Before an actor performs a dialogue, he or she must take the time to understand how the elements of a drama affect the meaning of the words to be said. The elements of a drama are explained on the next page. Complete the accompanying activities and take notes to use later as you prepare for your own performance.

1. **Plot** The plot of this scene from "Ride to the Hill" goes through three stages.

    Stage 1: Pauline takes out her frustrations about losing her horse on Martin.

    Stage 2: Pauline and Martin begin to become friends.

    Stage 3: Martin spoils things by hurting Pauline's feelings.

Find speeches that you think illustrate each of these three stages of the plot.

2. **Conflict** Pauline's feelings about losing Stanley create conflict at the beginning of the scene.
- Find a speech that shows conflict between Pauline and Martin caused by Pauline's feelings.
- Find a speech that shows that the conflict between Pauline and Martin seems to be resolved.
- Where in Martin's monologue on page 48 does a new source of conflict appear?

3. **Characters** With a partner, find speeches that answer each of the following questions about Pauline and Martin.
- What does Pauline want? What does Martin want?
- Does Pauline have any secrets she doesn't want Martin to know?
- Does Martin have any secrets he doesn't want Pauline to know?
- Do Pauline and Martin give away any of their secrets? If so, how?
- How do they feel about each other?
- How do these feelings change during the scene?

4. **Mood** The dramatist creates tension at the very beginning of the scene through Pauline's silences and her short answers to Martin's questions. Then the author adds to the tension by having Martin struggle to keep a conversation going.

Find speeches from the scene that signal changes in the mood.
- When does the tension between Pauline and Martin begin to relax?
- What other moods does the dialogue create?
- What is the mood at the end of the scene?

Discuss your examples with a partner.

5. **Climax** The peak of emotion occurs in Pauline's two speeches about being so tall (page 49).
- What effect do these speeches have on the mood of the scene?
- What do they show about Pauline's personality?

Work with a partner to experiment with different ways of reading Pauline's speeches. Try using a loud voice, and then a quiet but intense voice; try reading them quickly, and then with pauses. Think of other variations, or try combining different speeds and tones of voice. Which reading is the most effective? Why?

Preparing Your Performance

With a partner, prepare a Reader's Theatre performance of at least two full pages of dialogue from "Ride to the Hill." (Reader's Theatre is a stylized reading of a script that helps the audience visualize the drama.)

Decide which parts of the scene you found most interesting, and include at least one of these moments in your performance.

Use the notes you made earlier about the plot, conflict, characters, mood, and climax of the piece to help you prepare to perform your dialogue.

Follow the stage directions. Experiment with different ways of reading your lines to express your characters' emotions. Mark up your copy of the dialogue to suggest pauses, emphasis, changes in volume and speed, and so on. Be prepared to erase some markings and write new ones as you rehearse.

Try swapping roles with your partner to see if your partner's interpretation can show you something new about your lines.

Rehearse your lines until you feel completely comfortable with them. You can use a tape recorder to help you assess your performance and make improvements. (See Audiotaping on page 240.)

During your performance, make sure you speak clearly and slowly, so your audience can hear every word you say.

After your performance, ask your classmates to use the following checklist to assess your performance.

CHECKLIST: PERFORMING A DIALOGUE

✔ Could I hear and understand the entire performance?

✔ Was the performance well paced, neither too fast nor too slow?

✔ Did the performers clearly show the personalities of the characters they played?

✔ Did the performance add to my understanding of the scene?

✔ Which part of the performance did I like best?

✔ How might the performance have been improved?

Understanding Characters

You will interpret characters' words and actions to reach a better understanding of the characters in a drama.

Understanding the Task

Authors and scriptwriters use the following clues to tell you about characters in stories and dramas.

- **Words**: the kind of language the characters use, how they speak to other people, their values
- **Actions**: how the characters treat other people, how they behave under stress, the choices they make
- **Appearances**: the clothes the characters wear, how they take care of themselves
- **What Other People Say and Think:** how other characters treat them, how they speak to them and about them

However, sometimes characters don't say exactly what they mean, and you have to interpret their words and actions. For example, in "Ride to the Hill," Pauline doesn't come right out and say what she thinks of her father, but you can guess, or infer, Pauline's feelings from what she does say.

You can also figure out what a character feels or thinks by remembering your own experiences. Ask yourself

- How would I feel if that happened to me?
- How would my friends react in that situation?
- How have other characters in books and movies behaved in similar situations?

Interpreting the words and actions of characters can make reading stories and dramas far more interesting.

Getting Ready

Two excellent sources of clues to help you understand or interpret a character's words and actions are your personal experience and what the character says and does.

1. Personal Experience Reread pages 42–43. Although you don't know much about the characters yet, you can make some guesses about them based on what you know about people and what you would do if you were in the characters' shoes. How do you think Pauline will feel when she meets Martin?

Here are two possible predictions.
- She will be angry because Martin is taking Stanley away.
- She will be jealous because Martin is now Stanley's owner.

Is this how you would have answered the question? Why or why not?

Read between the lines and think about your own experience to answer this question: How do you think Martin might feel about meeting Pauline? Find a speech from the scene to support your answer.

2. **What the Character Says and Does** With a partner, discuss what the following speeches and stage directions reveal about how Pauline feels about herself and about her relationships with other people.

- "And when you try to ride him in the morning, he bucks." (page 44)

- "He [my father] says I'm making a fool of myself...because I've grown too big for him...and we look so funny together that people..." (page 46)

- "I'm sorry if you have to take a horse that you don't want." (page 46)

- "He knows all about me. All my secrets." (page 46)

- "Maybe there aren't as many [people], but the ones who are here can hurt you just as much." (page 49)

- Pauline smiles a gentle, forgiving smile, and hands him [Martin] the lead. (page 49)

Making a Character Web

A good way to organize your thoughts about a character is to make a web. Below is a partial character web for Pauline, using some quotations from the script. Words were then added to describe the character trait each quotation demonstrates.

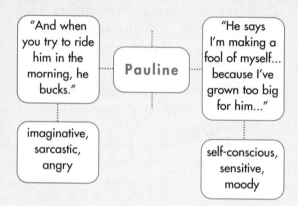

Work with a partner to complete the character web for Pauline and create one for Martin. Share your webs with those completed by another pair and compare the character traits you identified. A selection of descriptive words is provided in the Character Trait Word Bank on the next page, but feel free to use words not included in the Word Bank.

Interpreting Words and Actions

Use what you and your partner know about the character traits of Pauline and Martin to answer this question: Do you think that Pauline and Martin will become friends?

Collect examples from your character webs and quotations from the scene that suggest an answer to this question. You could use a chart to organize your thoughts.

With your partner, review your chart and draw a conclusion about whether or not Pauline and Martin will become friends. If you need some help deciding on your answer, consider these questions.
• What do they have in common?
• What might get in the way of their friendship?

Below your chart, write a few sentences to answer the question, and support your opinion with references to your chart.

When you have completed your chart, use the checklist on the next page to assess your work. You may wish to show your completed chart to classmates and have them use the checklist to assess your work.

Character Trait Word Bank

Stuck for words to describe characters? Try one of these.

abrupt, accomplished, adaptable, affectionate, aggressive, ambitious, angry, anxious, arrogant, artistic, awkward, blunt, boastful, calculating, cautious, changeable, competent, conceited, conscientious, consistent, courageous, creative, critical, cruel, cunning, curious, decisive, dependable, determined, dishonest, domineering, easy-going, eccentric, energetic, enthusiastic, fair, foolhardy, forgiving, frustrated, generous, gentle, gloomy, happy, helpful, humble, hypocritical, ill-tempered, imaginative, impatient, impolite, indecisive, inflexible, insecure, judgmental, just, loyal, meek, methodical, modest, moody, nervous, obstinate, open-minded, outgoing, outrageous, patient, persistent, proud, quarrelsome, resourceful, responsible, sarcastic, scatterbrained, secretive, self-conscious, selfish, sensitive, shrewd, sly, sophisticated, spontaneous, stubborn, superficial, tactful, timid, truthful, uncertain, uninhibited, unpredictable, weak, wise

Question: Will Pauline and Martin become friends?

Quotations	How They Answer the Question
Pauline: "And when you try to ride him in the morning, he bucks." (p. 44) Martin: "Don't have to. I'm so tough I just pick 'em up and carry 'em away." (p. 47)	Yes, they'll become friends because they both have good imaginations and a sense of humour.
Martin: "We'd probably be so worried about...how we'd look walking down the street together...." (p. 48)	No, they won't be friends because Martin has hurt Pauline's feelings.

CHECKLIST: UNDERSTANDING CHARACTERS

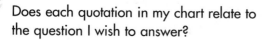

✓ Does each quotation in my chart relate to the question I wish to answer?

✓ Did I put the quotations from the teleplay in quotation marks?

✓ Did I explain how each quotation suggests an answer to the question?

✓ Did I draw on my personal experience to find an answer to the question?

✓ Does my final answer follow logically from the quotations in my chart?

✓ Did I express my ideas clearly?

Reading for Information

Reading for information is a very important part of learning, both at school and in your personal life. You read books and encyclopedias to find information for essays, or you read magazines to find out more about your favourite sport or band. Even when you browse the Internet or play video games, you have to read the information on the screen.

This unit offers strategies you can use to make sense of the information you read. These strategies may save you time when doing research and they may help you do better on tests. They might even help you read to understand better the world around you.

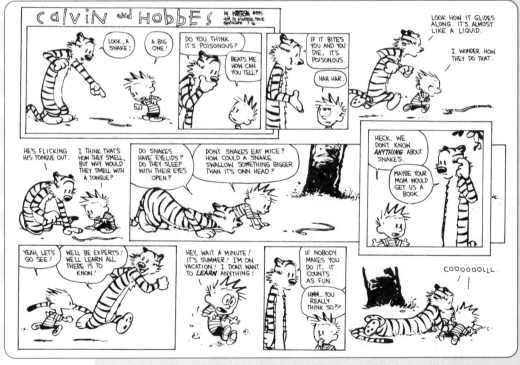

Reading Textbooks

LEARNING EXPECTATIONS
In this section, you will learn
- how textbooks help readers learn
- how to use a textbook to find the information you need
- how to take good notes
- how to read a textbook diagram

What Is a Textbook?

Textbooks are books written and designed to communicate information about a specific subject, such as algebra, biology, or geography. Textbooks contain information taken from many sources. Ideally, the information is well organized and clearly expressed so it can be understood easily.

The Elements of a Textbook

Textbooks use some specially designed elements that make for easier reading. Here are some of those elements.

Headings and Subheadings Each chapter of a textbook is divided into sections. The **heading** at the beginning of a section tells you what the topic is. The space at the end of a section shows you that the topic is finished

and a new one will follow. Sometimes a section is divided into smaller sections, each of which has its own **subheading**. On this page, "The Elements of a Textbook" is a heading and "Words That Jump Out" is a subheading. A textbook's table of contents often shows the headings and subheadings within each chapter.

Words That Jump Out Important words in textbooks are often emphasized so it's easy for you to find them. Look for words printed in **bold**, *italics*, or colour. These are the important words you are expected to understand. In some textbooks, you'll find important words listed in a glossary at the end of each chapter or at the end of the book.

Visuals Textbooks communicate information through words, but they also use **visuals**, such as photographs, diagrams, and charts. These visuals usually add information that you won't find in the written passages. Textbooks also use design elements, such as shaded boxes or illustrated borders, to draw your attention to special information.

Questions Many textbooks include **questions** at the end of sections or chapters. These questions ask you to show that you understand the information you've just read. Read the questions before you read the chapter and try to answer them as you read. If you don't know the answers, you should read that section or chapter again.

Overviews and Summaries Textbooks often list the most important ideas and words from a chapter in one paragraph or chart. This information might be at the beginning of a chapter, in an **introduction** or an **overview**. Or it might be at the end of a chapter, in a **summary** or **review**. You can use any of these elements to preview the information in a chapter, or as a study guide after you've read the chapter.

How to Read a Textbook

Here are some steps that will help you get the most from reading a textbook.
1. Divide the part of the textbook you must read into sections.
2. Look over one section to see which textbook elements are used.
3. Read all titles, headings, and subheadings, and skim for words that stand out. This step will help you to predict what you're about to read. For tips on how to skim, turn to page 111.
4. Read any questions included in the chapter.
5. Examine each visual carefully and read the titles or captions.
6. Take a moment to review the knowledge you already have about the topic.
7. Jot down some of your own questions to keep in mind as you read.
8. Read the section you have previewed.
9. Answer any questions provided at the end of the section. If necessary, reread the material so you can answer the questions.

For tips on how to skim, turn to page 111.

> **CRITICAL READING TIP**

Textbooks, like other kinds of writing, can be biased. But a bias in a textbook can be hard to see. To stay alert for hidden biases, ask yourself these questions.
- What views and ideas does the textbook present in a positive way? In a negative way?
- Does the textbook give a variety of perspectives on the ideas and issues it covers? Do some perspectives seem to be missing?
- Does the textbook raise the topic of bias? In what way?

The excerpt on the following pages is from a Canadian geography textbook. Work through steps 2–7 described on the left, and then read the excerpt, ignoring the notes in the margins. Note which textbook elements appear on these pages and look at how they are used. Then read the excerpt a second time, this time including the notes in the margins. When you have read the excerpt twice, work through the Tutorials on pages 64 and 67.

Water: Uses and Abuses

— from Krueger, Corder, Koegler, *This Land of Ours*. (Toronto: Harcourt Brace Canada, 1991)

SURPLUS OR SCARCITY?

"Canada has more fresh water per capita than any other country"
"Canada will face a water supply crisis before end of the century"

These two headlines appeared in a Canadian newspaper in the same year. How can they both be right?

A VALUABLE RESOURCE

In this chapter we look at Canada's freshwater resources: what they are and how important they are, and how we have used and abused them. ①

Water is one of our most valuable resources. All plants, animals, fish, and insects depend on water for their survival. As you answer the following questions, you will see how important water is to human beings.

1. Make a list of at least six ways you and your family use water in your home.

2. Tell why water is important to the following undertakings. ②
   a) livestock farming
   b) growing crops in dry regions
   c) the manufacture of steel, paper, and any two other products
   d) the production of electricity
   e) the transportation of bulky cargoes
   f) commercial and sport fishing
   g) recreational activities
   h) cleanliness

THE WATER CYCLE ③

Water that is available for human use is always on the move (Figure 6.1). It falls from clouds as rain or snow on land and sea. ④ Some of the **precipitation** that falls on land runs off. Passing through lakes, streams, and rivers, it finally reaches the ocean. The

---

1 This section shows me what the chapter will be about.

2 These points are easy. They want me to see how important water is.

3 I guess this is the next topic.

4 This term must be important. I'd better put it in my notes.

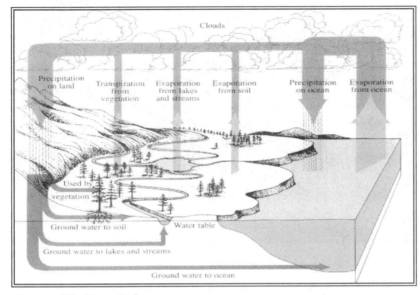

Figure 6.1 The Water Cycle

rest soaks into the ground. Some of the water that goes into the ground remains in the soil and subsoil, where it is used by plants. If there is enough precipitation, some water moves underground through layers of sand and gravel or porous rock to feed streams and lakes. Some of the underground water percolates deep, where it may remain until someone digs or drills a well to tap this source. If the land is near a seacoast, some of this ground water slowly works its way into the ocean.

As soon as precipitation reaches the surface, it starts making its way back up into the atmosphere. Some of it **evaporates** directly from the land and water surface. Plants begin at once to use any water that reaches them. Later they give off vast amounts of moisture into the atmosphere through a process called **transpiration**. The moisture released by evaporation and transpiration forms clouds. The clouds later return the moisture to earth, completing the water cycle.

Human actions often affect the movement of water in the water cycle. When forests are cut, water runs off the land more rapidly, and less water soaks into the ground. Water **run-off** increases even more when we build cities, where rain water quickly runs off roofs and paved surfaces. This increased run-off often has drastic results. Rapid run-off decreases the supply of ground water for plants, animals, and people. It also causes rivers to flood during wet periods

5 What does "porous" mean?

An urban area of high run-off **6**

6 There really isn't anywhere for the water to sink in. I wonder where it goes?

and streams to run dry during droughts. The following activities may make you even more aware of how much our actions alter the water cycle.

1. What happens to precipitation that falls on rooftops, streets, and parking lots? Where does it go from there? Compare its course with what happens to rain that falls on grass or treed areas.

2. Estimate the proportion of your schoolyard that is covered with asphalt or other material that water cannot penetrate. Do the same for the lot on which your home is located, and for a downtown block in your city or town (or the nearest city or town). How do these surfaces limit the amount of water available for human use in each of these areas?

CANADA'S WATER RESOURCES

The total amount of water on the earth has remained almost unchanged since the early days of the planet's history. Most of this water is sea water, too salty for our needs. Fresh water makes up **7** less than three percent of all the world's water, and most of that small proportion is not available for human use. Most of the world's fresh water is locked up in polar ice caps or lies deep underground beyond our reach. The available fresh water is stored in lakes and wetlands, and in the ground not far below the surface.

7 Is that still a lot of water?

Lakes and Wetlands **8**

Canada possesses a very generous share of the world's available fresh water. Though Canada has only one percent of the world's

8 This heading is smaller than the one above it. It must be a subheading.

population, it has nine percent of the fresh surface water supply. Much of this water is stored in lakes and wetlands such as **bogs**, **swamps**, **marshes**, and **sloughs**. These lakes and wetlands cover about twenty percent of Canada's surface. The list of Canadian lakes in Table 6.1 includes only the largest; you will find many thousands more on a large-scale map of Canada.

1. Locate in an atlas the lakes named in Table 6.1. Mark them on an outline map of Canada.

2. On your outline map, mark the southern edge of the Canadian Shield. Which of these lakes lie within (or partly within) the Canadian Shield?

3. Which provinces have none of the lakes listed in Table 6.1?

Table 6.1 Large Canadian Lakes

(Lakes covering more than 5000 km²)

Lake	Area (km²)
Superior*	84 500
Huron*	63 500
Great Bear	31 400
Great Slave	28 400
Erie*	25 800
Winnipeg	24 400
Ontario*	19 300
Athabasca	7 940
Reindeer	6 640
Nettilling	5 530
Winnipegosis	5 360

Source: The Inquiry on Federal Water Policy, *Currents of Change, Final Report*, 1985
*Note: These Great Lakes are shared with the United States.

9 I've never heard the names of a couple of these lakes. I wonder if I can find them in the atlas?

River Flow

Lakes and wetlands are important reservoirs. They store water, but by themselves they are not **renewable resources**. If a lake is drained, it stays dry until it is filled again by rivers that empty into it. For this reason, the number and size of lakes do not provide a good measurement of our renewable water supplies. A much better measurement is river flow. **10**

River flow depends on the amount of water run-off resulting from precipitation. As you would expect, the highest amount of water run-off in Canada occurs in British Columbia, where the precipitation is highest. Run-off rates are lowest in the southern prairie region, where there is much less precipitation. In this region there is no run-off at all in many years; the precipitation either evaporates or soaks into the ground. The volume of the river flow in any area is very difficult to measure because it varies from day to day and from month to month.

10 How do you measure river flow?

Taking Notes

LEARNING EXPECTATION
You will learn three note-taking methods and use one of them to write notes from a textbook passage.

Understanding the Task

When you take notes, you write a summary of information to use later. You will want to include the most information you can using the fewest words. To write useful notes, you have to decide which information is important and must be included, and which information can be left out.

Getting Ready

Here are some tips and techniques for note-taking. The tips give you some advice on what information to include in your notes. The techniques describe three ways of laying out your notes.

1. Note-Taking Tips To create good notes, you have to decide what information is important: this will depend on your reason for taking the notes. If you're studying for a test, your notes should probably be short, and focus on key terms. More detailed notes may be helpful when you're trying to understand a difficult topic. If you're gathering information for a presentation or an essay, you might take many pages of notes. Adjust your note-taking style to suit your purpose.

- Look for key terms. When you read a textbook, you are learning the key terms related to a single subject. These terms must appear in your notes. The following pointers will help you recognize key terms.
  - Words in special type (**bold**, *italics*, colour) are important—that's why they are highlighted.
  - Key terms often appear in titles, headings, subheadings, and captions.
  - Look for words that appear again and again throughout a paragraph, section, or chapter.
  - Key terms are often accompanied by definitions and examples.
  - Your own knowledge will help you to identify key terms. Trust your intuition.

Later in this Tutorial, you will learn different ways of structuring your notes around key terms.

- Use your own words whenever possible. When you express something in your own words, you have taken your first step towards understanding it. The notes that follow on the next page are based on the introductory paragraph to "Canada's Water Resources," on page 62.

> -most water on earth is salt w.
> -less than 3% fresh
> -some frozen, some far underground
> -use water from lakes, wetlands, and just
>   beneath ground level

- Be concise. Don't use full sentences. Numbers, symbols, abbreviations, and other short forms save space and increase your note-taking speed.

> Original Source   Note
> Though Canada has   - Can. 9%
> only one percent of   world's fresh
> the world's population,   surface water
> it has nine percent of
> the fresh surface water.

- Be neat and organized. When you read your notes later, you must be able to find the information you're looking for and understand what you've written.

2. Note-Taking Techniques Here are three different ways to lay out the notes you take as you read a textbook. The sample notes that follow are taken from pages 62–63 of the excerpt "Water: Uses and Abuses."

- **Point-Form Notes** This is a very common note-taking technique. Each key term or important idea is placed close to the left-hand margin. Support information follows in a series of brief phrases called **points**. Each point is indented on a new line and begins with

a hyphen (-) or a bullet (•). Use further indentation when you want to add information related to a specific point.

> world's water supply
>   - mostly sea water, too salty
>   - fresh water < 3%
>   - most locked in polar ice or undergr.
> Canada's fresh water
>   - 9% of world's fresh surface water
>   - stored in lakes & wetlands

This technique works well any time you need to take notes quickly.

- **Split-Page Notes** To create split-page notes, the page is divided into two columns—a narrow left-hand column and a wider right-hand column. Key terms and important ideas go on the left; supporting information goes on the right.

> world's water supply | - mostly sea water,
> | too salty
> | - fresh water < 3%
> | - most locked in polar
> | ice or undergr.

Because they have their own column, the key terms really stand out from the supporting information. Try this technique when you need to learn important terms or dates, or the names of people and places. You can list the key terms in the left column as a pre-reading activity, and fill in the right column as you read.

- **Mapping** Mapping is a more visual method of note-taking. Shapes such as boxes or circles emphasize key terms, while lines and arrows show how supporting information fits in. You might even use diagrams instead of words to represent some of the ideas.

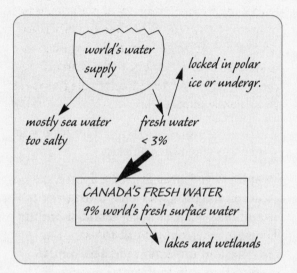

This technique works well if you like to see how things fit together, rather than read an explanation or description. Mapping takes more planning than the other techniques, so it's not good for quick note-taking. But it works well if you're studying for a test or preparing for a written assignment.

Writing Your Notes

Choose one or more of the three note-taking techniques and write notes from the information on pages 60–62 about the water cycle. Your notes should contain all the key terms, with supporting information for each term. When you've completed your notes, use the checklist below to assess your work.

Then choose a partner who has also completed this activity. Compare your notes with your partner's. Did you choose the same key terms and supporting information? Which note-taking technique did you use, and why did you choose it?

With your partner, discuss how to improve your notes. You might ask your partner to use the checklist to assess your notes.

CHECKLIST: TAKING NOTES

- ✔ Did I identify the key terms and use them to structure my notes?

- ✔ Did I include supporting information for each key term?

- ✔ Did I understand the information I included and use my own words wherever possible?

- ✔ Are my notes concise?

- ✔ Did I include words or information I didn't need?

- ✔ Did I leave out anything important?

- ✔ Are my notes neat and easy to follow?

Reading a Diagram

LEARNING EXPECTATION

○ You will learn how a diagram in a text-book communicates information and you will use your knowledge to change a diagram to make it easier to read.

Diagrams are one of the most complex types of visuals to appear in textbooks. This Tutorial shows you several strategies you can use to help you read a diagram. You can also use these strategies to design better diagrams for your own assignments.

Understanding the Task

Sometimes a complicated idea can be communicated more easily when a diagram, graph, chart, or other illustration appears with the words. That is why textbooks generally include so many diagrams and other illustrations.

Getting Ready

Here are a few strategies to help you read a textbook diagram. Below is a diagram that appeared on page 61 of the textbook excerpt. The numbers have been added to refer to the reading strategies described on the next page.

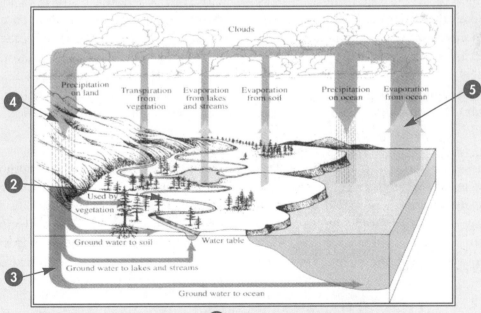

Figure 6.1 The Water Cycle

1. Start with the title. The title tells you what the illustration is about. It may also use a word or phrase from the text to show you which paragraph the diagram belongs with. In this diagram, the title also includes a **figure number**, "Figure 6.1." As you can see, the figure number is mentioned in the last paragraph on page 60. This is the best way to connect a diagram to the related information in the text.

2. Study the picture carefully. See if you recognize the details in the picture. The details in Figure 6.1 show land and water, with mountains on the left and the ocean on the right, as well as trees, clouds, and rivers. When you see a picture that you don't understand, read the text near the diagram to find an explanation of the information in the diagram. Use the figure number, or the title and key words from the caption of the diagram, to find related information in the text.

3. Read all the labels. Each label has a purpose. In a well-designed diagram, it is easy to identify which part of the illustration each label refers to. Read the text again if you don't understand a label. The most important labels are often larger or printed in CAPITAL LETTERS or **bold type**.

4. Follow the arrows. Arrows are an important part of many diagrams. They are used to show movement and direction, or they may connect labels to the things they name. In Figure 6.1, the arrows show how water moves through the stages of the water cycle.

5. Look for the use of shading, colour, or symbols. The designer of Figure 6.1 used shading in two ways. First, shading helps to separate the mountains from the land, and the land from the ocean. Second, the way the arrows are shaded helps you to see the difference between evaporation and precipitation. Some diagrams have a **key** or a **legend** that shows how shading, colour, or symbols are used.

TECHNOLOGY TIP

You can create your own diagrams with a computer graphics package. It's easy to experiment with size, colour, typefaces, borders, and labels on a computer.

Making a Diagram Easier to Read

Is the diagram on page 69 as easy to read as it could be? Use the five strategies above to read and assess the diagram. Make a note of any problems you notice or any questions you have about the diagram. Then work with a partner to suggest changes that will make it easier to read. Read the explanation given beside the diagram to help you decide how to improve the diagram itself.

With your partner, draw the diagram with the changes you have suggested. When your diagram is complete, use the checklist below to assess your work. Show your diagram to someone who has not completed this activity. Ask that person to assess your diagram using the same checklist.

What's wrong with this diagram?

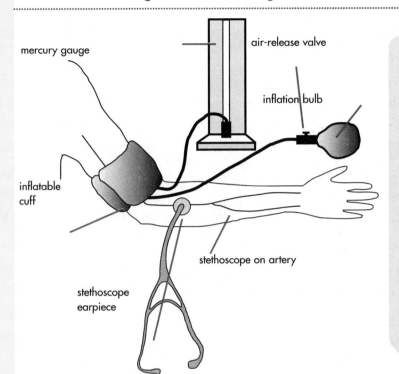

mercury gauge

air-release valve

inflation bulb

inflatable cuff

stethoscope on artery

stethoscope earpiece

Explanation: The diagram shows how to measure blood pressure. The bulb, cuff, and gauge are one instrument. Air from the bulb inflates the cuff. As the cuff inflates, the mercury rises in the gauge. The inflated cuff reduces the flow of blood through the artery. The flow of blood can be heard through the stethoscope.

CHECKLIST: READING A DIAGRAM

✓ Does my diagram have a clear title?

✓ Are the details of my diagram easy to see and identify?

✓ Are the labels easy to read? Do they clearly connect to the details they name and not interfere with the picture?

✓ Did I use shading, colours, and arrows to make the diagram easy to follow?

✓ Is the information in my diagram easy to understand?

Reading News Articles

What Is a News Article?

A **news article**, also called a **news story**, or just a **story**, tells you about a real-life event, usually one that happened recently or is still going on. News articles present a lot of information very quickly. Here is a sample news article with its important elements labelled.

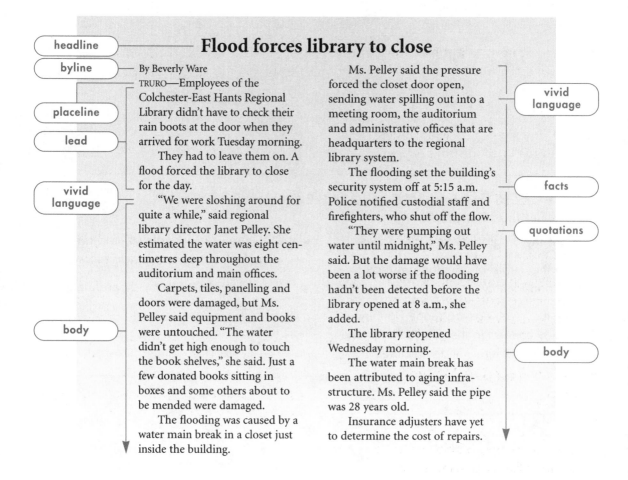

Flood forces library to close

headline
byline

By Beverly Ware

placeline
lead

TRURO—Employees of the Colchester-East Hants Regional Library didn't have to check their rain boots at the door when they arrived for work Tuesday morning.

vivid language

They had to leave them on. A flood forced the library to close for the day.

"We were sloshing around for quite a while," said regional library director Janet Pelley. She estimated the water was eight centimetres deep throughout the auditorium and main offices.

Carpets, tiles, panelling and doors were damaged, but Ms. Pelley said equipment and books were untouched. "The water didn't get high enough to touch the book shelves," she said. Just a few donated books sitting in boxes and some others about to be mended were damaged.

body

The flooding was caused by a water main break in a closet just inside the building.

Ms. Pelley said the pressure forced the closet door open, sending water spilling out into a meeting room, the auditorium and administrative offices that are headquarters to the regional library system.

vivid language

The flooding set the building's security system off at 5:15 a.m. Police notified custodial staff and firefighters, who shut off the flow.

facts

"They were pumping out water until midnight," Ms. Pelley said. But the damage would have been a lot worse if the flooding hadn't been detected before the library opened at 8 a.m., she added.

quotations

The library reopened Wednesday morning.

The water main break has been attributed to aging infrastructure. Ms. Pelley said the pipe was 28 years old.

body

Insurance adjusters have yet to determine the cost of repairs.

The Elements of a News Article

The important information in a news article is highlighted by elements such as these.

Headline It catches your eye and sums up the story.

Byline It tells you who wrote the article, and sometimes gives the journalist's specialty, for example, "Science Reporter."

Placeline It tells you where the story originates.

Lead It briefly gives the most important information.

Body It supplies additional information. Notice how the body is divided into short paragraphs, each introducing a new piece of information.

Facts Every news article includes simple, true statements about what happened, such as "The flooding set the building's security system off at 5:15 a.m."

Vivid Language Journalists use words to create interest and make you feel as if you saw the event yourself.

Quotations These retell, word for word, what someone actually said, adding accuracy and an "at-the-scene" feeling.

How to Read a News Article

Here are some tips to help you get the most information from a newspaper article.

1. Start by examining the headline, byline, photographs, and captions. What do they tell you about the story? Think about what you already know about the people, places, and events mentioned.

2. Jot down some questions you think the article should answer. Return to these questions after you've read the article to see if any questions remain unanswered.

3. If you don't recognize a name in a news article, go back to the beginning of the article and scan forward until you find the first time the name is mentioned. You'll see the full name and an explanation of who the person is.

4. Journalists put the least important details at the end of the article so readers won't miss much if they don't finish the article. Don't read to the end if you think you've got the main information you want. But it may be worth reading the last couple of paragraphs. The conclusion may add an interesting point.

The news article "9.84" appears on the following pages. Read the article once, ignoring the notes in the margins. As you read, follow the four steps described above. Jot down any thoughts or questions that occur to you as you read.

Then read the article again, this time including the notes in the margins. Compare the margin notes to the notes you made as you read. When you've read the article a second time, work through the Tutorials on pages 75 and 78.

1 What does the headline mean? Oh, it's a time!

2 I like the way the picture and the headline say it all!

3 He makes it sound like Bailey didn't stand a chance. I guess the "experts" were wrong!

Ottawa Citizen   **SPORTS**   July 28, 1996

9.84 ①

② *Donovan Bailey blows away world record — and memory of Ben Johnson*

CAM COLE
Southam Olympic Team

ATLANTA—World's Fastest Human. Donovan Bailey wore that title for a year after winning his 1995 world championship, but nobody really believed it.

He was the one-shot wonder who never took training seriously, who had come out of nowhere and—so the experts believed—was destined to return there at these Olympic Games.

But when the men's 100-metre final—the Olympics' No. 1 glamor event—threatened to come apart at the seams Saturday night, guess who didn't flinch? When the field had to start over three times, guess who still had gas in the tank?

When the defending Olympic champ, Linford Christie, was disqualified after his second false start, guess who wasn't fazed? And when Christie and Trinidad's Ato Boldon nearly came to blows in the back rooms of Centennial Olympic Stadium after the race, while Dennis Mitchell was decrying it as "the most unprofessional race I've ever seen in my life," guess who was out on the track, doing a victory lap with the Canadian flag held aloft?

The World's Fastest Human, that's who.

4 Donovan Bailey blew away one of the most powerful fields in the history of the 100 metres with a massive kick at the 50-metre mark that powered him from fifth place to first—and won the Olympic gold medal in a world record time of 9.84 seconds, 1-100th of a second faster than the old standard owned by American Leroy Burrell.

"I wasn't thinking world record," said Bailey, "because every time I go into a race thinking about a time, I screw it up. All I was thinking about was relaxing, and when I led at 70 metres, I knew I had it and all I had to do was relax and take it home."

Now, perhaps, at last, the ghost of Ben Johnson can be put to rest.

"Let's see now," an American reporter said to Bailey later, "Canadian sprinter, born in Jamaica, wins Olympic gold medal in world record time. Why does this sound familiar?"

Bailey knew the question was coming, because it always does.

"I'm not trying to undo what Ben did in Seoul," said the 28-year-old from Oakville, Ont.

"You know, my name is Donovan Bailey. No matter what happens in history, it's always going to come up, every sprint, not just me—but me most of all because I'm Canadian and I'm from Jamaica."

But few believe this is Ben Johnson II. They're not even close in personality. Bailey is outgoing, friendly, always smiling. 5

And he smiled right through three rounds of racing leading up to the final, even 6 though he had appeared to be on the second tier, as everyone else was compared to Namibia's Frankie Fredericks and Trinidad's Ato Boldon.

"I wasn't playing possum, 7 I don't believe in that," said Bailey. "I just had to run my own races, every round. And I ran it in the final, and wound up with a gold medal—and a world record."

He won despite being dead-last out of the blocks, he won after appearing to trail the field dangerously as late as 30 or 40 metres into the race. 8

"I knew my start wasn't the best," said Bailey, "but my finishes were."

He won, too, despite the distractions of three false starts, and Christie's refusal to leave the track after he was disqualified.

4 This is an exciting description of the race.

5 The reporter thinks Bailey is a nice guy.

6 Now it's like we're at the finish line right after the race is over.

7 I don't know what a possum is but I think I understand what Bailey is saying.

8 Bailey was fantastic. I saw the race.

Fredericks, who, along with Boldon, had seemed to be on a whole different plane through three qualifying rounds—they ran 9.93 and 9.94, respectively, in the semifinals—had to come between Christie and Boldon when the two nearly began throwing punches after the race.

9 Which one is Linford? I have to look back.

"I have a lot of respect for Linford," Boldon said, "but he should have left the track. And I think my inexperience let all the goings-on affect me. It was my fault.

"Donovan was the best man out there today, but I let it get to me."

"I think that just allowed me to relax a bit more," said Bailey. "I didn't even know what was going on. Was Linford disqualified?"

Presumably, he was kidding —nobody's that focused. But Bailey said he wasn't even aware of the bomb that exploded in Centennial Olympic Park the night before until he awoke late Saturday morning, and clearly he hadn't been briefed on the details yet.

10 Wow! He must have been in a deep sleep!

"I think it's crazy, these idiots, these lunatics," Bailey said. "My heart goes out to the people who got hurt. I hope everybody's all right."

Later, asked by a Jamaican reporter how he felt about the country of his birth sharing his victory, Bailey said: "Well, I'm Jamaican, man. I was born there, that's a fact. So I'm a Jamaican-born Canadian sprinter who loves his adopted country."

That became clear during the playing of the national anthem as Bailey struggled to hold back tears, eventually turning his head away from the cameras to wipe his eyes.

The evening didn't go nearly so well for Canada's other top-ranked sprinter. Bruny Surin's goose was cooked before the gun went off for his semi-final heat.

He was drawn against five very tough sprinters and was clearly off form all through this competition. There didn't look to be any way the Montreal veteran could win through to the final—and there wasn't. In the end, his best time of the 1996 Olympic games was a mediocre 10.13, and at age 29, you have to believe Atlanta will be the end of the line.

A guy who spent so much of his best years in the shadow of Ben deserved a better fate. But maybe, with Donovan Bailey's win Saturday, that shadow will go away, at last.

11 I liked the beginning of the article best because it was more exciting.

Analyzing a News Article

LEARNING EXPECTATIONS
- You will analyze how a news article is organized, identifying the lead and the body.
- You will determine whether the article answers the W5 + H questions, and you will create a summary of the information the article contains.

Understanding the Task

When writing a news article, a journalist must
- answer the questions readers might have about the story
- provide the answers in an obvious way so they can be found easily

Journalists are taught to recognize the questions readers are most likely to ask. They are also taught how to present information in an organized way. Knowing how news articles are organized may help you find information more easily for research assignments.

Getting Ready

When you analyze a story, you break it down and look at the parts used to create the story. In a news article, you would look at three things: the questions the article answers; the lead to the article; and the body of the article, where the information is presented.

1. **The Questions** The abbreviation **W5 + H** refers to the six questions every news article must answer. Readers want to know
- **Who** did it?
- **What** happened?
- **When** did it happen?
- **Where** did it happen?
- **Why** did it happen?
- **How** did it happen?

Notice that the journalist who wrote "9.84" answers all six questions.

Questions	Answers
Who did it?	"Donovan Bailey" (paragraph 1)
What happened?	"won the Olympic gold medal in a world record time of 9.84 seconds" (paragraph 6)
When did it happen?	"Saturday night" (paragraph 3)
Where did it happen?	"these Olympic Games" (paragraph 2; see the placeline too)
Why did it happen?	"didn't flinch...still had gas in the tank" (paragraph 3)
How did it happen?	"a massive kick at the 50-metre mark that powered him from fifth place to first" (paragraph 6)

2. The Lead Cole answers four of the six questions in the first three paragraphs of "9.84." This is typical of news articles. They have strong starts, with the most crucial information packed into the first few sentences. This opening section is known as the **lead**. It can be as short as one paragraph, but may be much longer. The lead doesn't have to answer all the W5 + H questions, but it should answer the most important ones, usually *who, what, where,* and *when.*

In "9.84," the lead is six paragraphs long. Cole can wait to answer *what* and *how* because he knows this is one story that most people will read to the end. Also, the reader already knows what happened from seeing the headline and the photograph.

The lead often contains a **hook** that grabs the reader's attention and keeps him or her reading. Unanswered questions, controversial statements, and exciting events are some common forms of the hook. Cole uses a couple of hooks. He describes Donovan Bailey as a "one-shot wonder" (paragraph 2), knowing that people love to read about underdogs who become champions. Can you see the other hook? Here's a hint: it appears in the second part of the headline and is mentioned in the middle and at the end of the article.

3. The Body After the lead comes the **body** of the article. It contains more details, but the information becomes less important the further you read. Journalists use this pattern, called the **inverted pyramid**, so that readers won't miss anything important if they don't read to the end of the article.

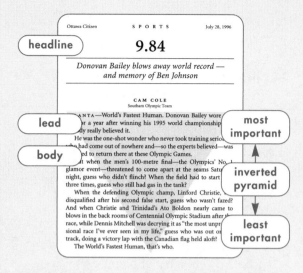

You can see this structure quite clearly in "9.84." Most readers will be looking for a description of the race, and Cole has provided it by the end of the sixth paragraph. Cole uses the remaining 23 paragraphs to add more details.

Details	Paragraph #
Bailey's perspective	7
Ben Johnson issue	8–13
Bailey's performance in heats	14–15
more about the race	16–17
effects of the false starts	18–22
the Olympic bombing	23–24
Bailey's Jamaican heritage	25
Bailey's patriotism	26
Bruny Surin's performance	27–29

Writing Your Analysis

Now you can apply what you've learned. Read the news article on the next page, "DNA traces teacher's lineage back 9000 years," and analyze it, following these four steps.

1. Identify where the lead begins and ends.
2. Using a chart like the one on page 75, show how the article answers the W5 + H questions.
3. Using a chart like the one on page 76, create a summary of the details in the body of the article.
4. In your opinion, does the body of the article follow the inverted pyramid structure?

Once you have finished your analysis, work with a partner to compare your results. Then assess your work using the checklist below. Discuss any differences in your analyses, and try to reach agreement.

DNA traces teacher's lineage back 9000 years

Associated Press

LONDON—Using DNA from a tooth, scientists have established a blood tie between a 9000-year-old skeleton known as Cheddar Man and an English schoolteacher who lives near the cave where the bones were found.

Oxford University scientists announced yesterday that Adrian Targett, 42, a history teacher in Cheddar in southwestern England, shares a common ancestor with Cheddar Man.

It is the longest human lineage ever traced, the team of scientists from the university's Institute of Molecular Medicine said.

"I am overwhelmed, a bit surprised," said Targett, who ancestry was revealed during the filming of a documentary for the TV station HTV, which commissioned the study. "I was just about to say I hope it's not me."

Dr. Larry Barham, a Texas-born archeologist at Bristol University, said the finding "adds to the evidence that Britons came from a race of hunter-gatherers who later turned to farming because they found it was to their advantage." Archeologists believe Cheddar Man, who lived during the Stone Age, was a hunter-gatherer.

CHECKLIST: ANALYZING A NEWS ARTICLE

✓ Did I identify the paragraphs that formed the lead?

✓ Was the lead effective? If not, how could it be improved?

✓ Did I find the answers to all the W5 + H questions? How many were in the lead?

✓ Did I think the article gave the reader enough information about the story?

✓ What questions were left unanswered?

✓ Did the writer use a hook to grab my attention? Where and how often does the hook appear in the article?

Seeing the Slant

LEARNING EXPECTATION
You will compare two news articles that cover the same event, identifying the different slant taken by each one. You will also discuss how far slant should go.

Understanding the Task

Journalists must work to keep your attention while telling you the facts. One way they do this is by giving a news article a **slant**. The slant of a news article is the same as its main idea. To develop a slant, the journalist chooses and arranges the facts to express a certain point of view.

Here's an example. Imagine there's a new cafeteria opening in your school. One journalist might decide that the story should focus on cost issues. Her article could explore the expense of the new equipment, how much the food will cost, and the price of food at a nearby restaurant. Another journalist might focus on the quality of the food. He could write about the variety of foods, how well the food is prepared, and whether the meals are nutritious. Both stories are about the cafeteria opening. They might even use some of the same details. But each one has its own slant, so each one will have a different effect on the readers.

Getting Ready

Would it surprise you to learn that "9.84" has a very strong slant? Perhaps you didn't notice it because the journalist expresses a point of view that you share! But if you put two headlines about the same event side by side, the slant becomes more obvious.

OTTAWA CITIZEN

9.84
Donovan Bailey
blows away world record—
and memory of Ben Johnson

WASHINGTON POST

Bailey Sets Mark in 100
Joyner-Kersee Out
of Heptathlon

Compare "blows away world record" with "sets mark." The first phrase, from a Canadian headline, is full of emotion; the second phrase, from a U.S. headline, is not. By looking at the two headlines, you can see that the Canadian article is more pro-Bailey than the American article.

Now look at how the two articles describe Bailey's victory.

Donovan Bailey blew away one of the most powerful fields in the history of the 100 metres with a massive kick at the 50-metre mark that powered him from fifth place to first—and won the Olympic gold medal in a world record time of 9.84 seconds, 1-100th of a second faster than the old standard owned by American Leroy Burrell.

OTTAWA CITIZEN

Bailey, who was born in Jamaica, broke the two-year-old mark of American Leroy Burrell by one-hundredth of a second. The last time a Canadian crossed the finish line first in the men's 100 at the Olympics, he also was Jamaican-born and a new world record holder. It was Ben Johnson. Three days later, he was banned from the 1988 Seoul Olympics for a positive drug test and stripped of his medal and his record.

WASHINGTON POST

The Canadian article builds up Bailey's victory by using words that emphasize his abilities—"blew away," "most powerful fields," "massive kick," "powered him." The U.S. article, on the other hand, takes away from Bailey's achievement by raising the shadow of Ben Johnson's disqualification.

The chart below shows that the story of Bailey's victory is a very minor part of the U.S. article.

	"9.84"	"Bailey Sets Mark"
# of paragraphs in article	29	28
# of paragraphs about Bailey	24	3
# of paragraphs about others in the race	5	4
# of paragraphs about other events	0	21

You can see that the slant of the Canadian article is very different from the slant of the American article. It's not surprising that a Canadian paper would have this slant. And once you're aware of the slant in "9.84," it's easy to find many words and phrases that encourage the reader to see Bailey as a hero. The first sentence—"World's Fastest Human"—is a perfect example.

Make a list of words and phrases in "9.84" that glorify Donovan Bailey. Compare your list with someone else's. Did you choose the same examples?

How Far Should a Slant Go?

The slant in "9.84" makes it more interesting to read, but it also makes it less objective. Cole doesn't just present the facts; he interprets them. He encourages the reader to see the race from his point of view. In other words, "9.84" is **biased**.

All news articles are biased to some degree, because they are shaped by the interests and values of the journalists and editors who create them. As a reader, you must watch for bias and assess its effects. Few readers will accept a news article that gives lies instead of facts, but most will accept a gentle bias, especially if they happen to agree.

What do you think? Is the slant in "9.84" acceptable? Or has Cole gone too far? Discuss your answers with a group of classmates. Working together, add as many examples as you can to the following list of possible slants or biases. Then answer the questions below.

Slant or Bias	Example
ageism	The protesters, mostly teenagers, destroyed property around city hall.
nationalism	The Canadian rower came in second; the winner passed her only in the last metre of the race.
bias against Hollywood films	It was a typical Hollywood flick, full of action and special effects, but with no real story.

- What kinds of bias might be acceptable in a news story? Why?
- What kinds of bias might be acceptable in a sports, fashion, or entertainment story? Why?
- In general, when should bias be avoided, and when can it be allowed? Explain your answer.

For more information about bias and how to detect it, turn to page 114.

Seeing the Slant for Yourself

You should be able to describe the slant of an article in one sentence. The slant of "9.84" might be described like this: "Donovan Bailey became a Canadian sports hero when he blew away the competition at the 1996 Olympics."

On the next page are the opening paragraphs from two articles about another race at the 1996 Olympics. Follow these steps to analyze the slant.

1. Read the first excerpt and list the words and phrases that suggest a slant. Repeat this step for the second excerpt.
2. Write a sentence describing what you think the slant of the first article is. Do the same thing for the second excerpt.
3. Reread both articles and revise the two slants you wrote in step 2, if necessary.
4. Discuss your conclusions with a partner. Was one slant easier to sum up than the other? Do you think one article has a stronger slant?

When you've completed your analysis, compare your results with those of a partner who has finished the same activity. With your partner, assess your work, using the checklist on the next page. Were your descriptions of the slants for the two excerpts similar? Can you explain any differences?

Perfect 10 goes to Canadians
Minus Lewis, US men stunned; women bring home relay gold

By Joe Concannon

ATLANTA—Oh, Canada. The Canadian team that was all but forgotten in the wake of the Carl Lewis controversy buried the US 4x100 meter relay team last night, as anchor Donovan Bailey, the gold medalist and world record-holder in the 100, was given the perfect pass from Bruny Surin and he took it home for the gold medal.

This marked the first time in either Olympic or world championship history that the United States had been beaten in this race when the team crossed the finish line. The Canadian team of Robert Esmie, Glenroy Gilbert, Surin and Bailey won in history's sixth-fastest time of 37.69. Dennis Mitchell ran the last leg but had no chance given Bailey's speed. The US finished in 38.05 and Brazil took the bronze (38.41).

BOSTON GLOBE

Fantastic Four steal show from smug U.S. relay team

By Doug Smith

ATLANTA—It was about more than just gold, it was about respect.

The Canadian men's 4x100 metre relay team blitzed a group of cocky Americans to win the Olympic gold medal and strike a blow against the xenophobia that's run rampant here at the Atlanta games.

"There was absolutely no mention that we were the world champions, that there were a couple of guys from up north who could win this," said Donovan Bailey of Oakville, Ont., who anchored Saturday's triumph and crossed the finish line with his arm high in exultation, another little dig at the second-place Americans.

"I don't think we got as much respect as we should. We were on a mission."

Bailey, along with Robert Esmie of Sudbury, Ont., a brilliant Glenroy Gilbert of Ottawa and Montreal's Bruny Surin, accomplished the near impossible with the 37.69-second race: They turned dozens of American journalists into fans —who were cheering against the United States.

HALIFAX CHRONICLE-HERALD

CHECKLIST: SEEING THE SLANT

✓ Did I express each slant clearly, in my own words?

✓ Did I identify words and phrases that suggest the two slants?

✓ Do I think the slant is okay, or has either of the writers gone too far?

✓ Is there any part of the article that departs from the slant or suggests another point of view?

Reading Opinion Pieces

LEARNING EXPECTATIONS
In this section, you will learn
- what an opinion piece is
- how to tell a fact from an opinion
- how writers can manipulate your feelings and opinions
- how to read an opinion piece critically and assess the effectiveness of a writer's arguments

What Is an Opinion Piece?

Opinions are strongly held beliefs. Although it's impossible to prove that an opinion is absolutely true or false, it is possible to support and recommend an opinion. That is what a writer does in an **opinion piece**.

An opinion piece is one kind of **persuasive writing**. It is an essay in which the writer expresses an opinion and then explains or defends it. Opinion pieces are found in most magazines and newspapers.

The Elements of an Opinion Piece

There are three elements that all opinion pieces must have.

1. A Strong Statement of Opinion This often appears in a single sentence close to the beginning of the piece. In the sample paragraph below, the statement of opinion is in sentence 1.

2. A Context The writer must show why the opinion expressed is important to the writer or why it should be important to the reader. The context may be openly stated, or it may be implied throughout the selection, as in the sample. You could summarize the context of the sample paragraph this way: Society pays when young people choose the wrong career.

How to Choose a Career

(1) At fifteen, students should be told what career to pursue based on their school performance. (2) Most students are confused about what career to choose. (3) They need to be told what to do. (4) When students choose a career themselves, they usually pick one they don't know much about. (5) When they get a job, they discover they don't like it; then all their education and training is wasted. (6) If careers were assigned instead of chosen, society would always have the right number of workers. (7) Unemployment would decrease and job satisfaction would be higher. (8) And taxpayers would know that money going to education was being well spent.

3. Support for the Opinion A writer can use facts to support an opinion. But he or she can also use other kinds of support, such as general observations (sentence 2); predictions about future effects of an action (sentence 6); and appeals to the reader's interests (sentences 7 and 8).

How to Read an Opinion Piece

Beware! The writer of an opinion piece wants you to accept his or her point of view. To accomplish this goal, the writer might present clear arguments and support them with facts. However, the writer might use some facts while omitting others, or use a friendly tone just to win your trust.

You can resist this manipulation by being a **critical reader**. Reading critically does not mean looking only for weaknesses, tricks, and errors; it means asking questions and looking for your own answers. Look at the questions a critical reader might have about the opinion in the paragraph on page 82.

Sentence 1: Whose point of view is being expressed here?

Sentence 3: Is this the only solution?

Sentence 5: Is this statement true?

Sentence 6: Who makes the choice?

Sentence 8: Is job placement the main purpose of education?

Every piece of writing expresses an opinion or an underlying **bias**, so it's important to read critically all the time. Ask yourself what the writer's point of view is and why.

Compare it with your own and with other people's. This unit will help you to become a more critical reader.

An opinion piece entitled "Do We Need to Use Animals in Research?" appears on the following pages. Before you read it, follow these steps to prepare.

1. Read the title.
2. On a separate piece of paper, create and fill in a chart like the one below.

Do We Need to Use Animals in Research?	
Reasons for saying yes • •	*Reasons for saying no* • •

3. Looking at the reasons you've written, how would you answer the question asked in the title? Write your answer underneath the chart you made.

Now read the opinion piece, ignoring the notes in the margins. Identify the statement of opinion and the context for the opinion. Is there anything you should add to your chart? Then reread the opinion piece, this time including the margin notes. Did the opinion piece give the same answer to the question in the title that you did? If not, did the piece change your mind?

When you have read the selection twice, work through the Tutorials on pages 87 and 91.

1 I guess the opinion piece will answer this question.

DO WE NEED TO USE Animals

IN RESEARCH? ①

There are only about 10,000 people with CF in the United States. But the number of people dependent on research is much larger.

JANE McCABE

i see the debate about using animals in medical research in stark terms. If you had to choose between saving a very cute dog or my equally cute, blond, brown-eyed daughter, **2** whose life would you choose? It's not a difficult choice, is it? My daughter has cystic fibrosis. Her only hope for a normal life is that researchers, some of them using animals, will find a cure. Don't misunderstand. It's not that I don't love animals, it's just that I love Claire more.

Nine years ago I had no idea that I would be joining the fraternity of those who have a vital interest in seeing that medical research continues. I was a very pregnant woman in labor; with my husband beside me I gave birth to a 7-pound,

2 Of course I'd save the girl. Why is she asking me this question?

1-ounce [3200-g] daughter. It all seemed so easy. But for the next four months she could not gain weight. She was a textbook case of failure to thrive. Finally a hospital test of the salt content in her sweat led to the diagnosis of cystic fibrosis.

The doctor gave us a little reason for hope. "Your daughter will not have a long life, but for most of the time, it will be a good life. Her life expectancy is about 13 years, though it could be longer or shorter. As research continues, we're keeping them alive longer."

"As research continues." It's not a lot to rely on but what's our alternative? We haven't waited passively. We learned

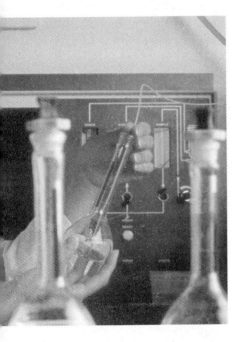

how to take care of our little girl; her medical problems affect her digestion and lungs. We protected her from colds, learned about supplemental vitamins and antibiotics. We moved to California where the winters aren't so harsh and the

cold and flu season isn't so severe. Our new doctor told us that the children at his center were surviving, on the average, to age 21. So far, our daughter is doing well. She is a fast runner and plays a mean first base. She loves her friends and is, in general, a happy little girl. All things considered, I feel very lucky.

How has research using animals helped those with CF? Three times a day my daughter uses enzymes from the pancreas of pigs to digest her food. She takes antibiotics tested on rats before they are tried on humans. As an adult, she will probably develop diabetes and need insulin—a drug developed by research on dogs and rabbits. If she ever needs a heart-lung transplant, one might be possible because of the cows that surgeons practiced on. There is no animal model to help CF research, but once the CF gene is located, new gene-splicing techniques may create a family of mice afflicted with the disease. Researchers would first learn to cure the mice with drugs, then cautiously try with humans.

There are only about 10 000 people with CF in the United States. But the number of people dependent on research is much larger. Walk with me

3 I feel sorry for the girl and her parents.

4 I didn't know they used animals so much in research. Are these animals killed for this research? Is there research that doesn't use animals?

5 Those children need help. Research is important.

6 She doesn't talk much about the animals. It's like she doesn't want me to think about them.

7 This is getting pretty emotional!

8 What about other kinds of research, like testing shampoo and make-up?

through Children's Hospital at Stanford University: here are the youngsters fighting cancer, **5** rare genetic illnesses, immunological diseases. Amid their laughter and desperate attempts to retain a semblance of child- **6** hood, there is suffering.

I think the motivation of animal-rights activists is to cut

Every time I see a bumper sticker that says "Lab animals never have a nice day," a fantasy plays in my brain. I get out of my car, tap on the driver's window and ask to talk. In my fantasy, the other driver gets out, we find a coffee shop and I show her photos of my kids. I ask her if she has ever visited

Why is a laboratory rat's fate more poignant than that of an incurably ill child?

down on the suffering in this world, but I have yet to hear them acknowledge that people —young and old—suffer, too. **7** Why is a laboratory rat's fate more poignant than that of an incurably ill child?

There are advocates for animals who only seek to cut down on "unnecessary research." They don't specify how to decide what is unnecessary, but they do create an atmosphere in which doing medical research **8** is seen as distasteful work. I think that's wrong. Researchers should be thanked, not hassled.

Children's Hospital. I am so eloquent that her eyes fill with tears and she promises to think of the children who are wasting away as she considers the whole complicated issue of suffering.

I have other fantasies, too, that a cure is found for what ails my daughter, that she marries and gives us some grandchildren, and does great work in her chosen profession, which at this moment appears to be cartooning or computer programming. We can still hope—as long as the research continues.

Facts and Opinions

LEARNING EXPECTATION
You will identify facts and opinions in an opinion piece. You will also generate an argument that includes facts and opinions.

Understanding the Task

When you read an opinion piece, you want to be able to tell the strong arguments from the weak. Since a strong argument is built upon facts, you need to know what a fact is and how it differs from an opinion. And when you come to write your own arguments, you'll need to be able to support your personal opinions with facts that convince your readers.

Getting Ready

A **fact** is a statement that can be proved to be true. Here's an example: "The earth orbits the sun." If a statement is really a fact, you can't disagree with it. But you *can* disagree with which facts the writer chooses and which ones he or she ignores.

An **opinion**, on the other hand, is a statement that expresses a belief or point of view that cannot be proved one way or the other. "The earth is the most beautiful planet in the solar system." Although many people might

agree with this statement, there are many who would not. Some might say, "Saturn is the most beautiful planet because of its rings." Others might say, "All the planets are equally beautiful, but in different ways." An opinion is always open to debate.

Here are two quotations from "Do We Need to Use Animals in Research?" Which quotation is a fact and which is an opinion?

1. "I think the motivation of animal-rights activists is to cut down on the suffering in this world...."

2. "There are only about 10 000 people with CF in the United States."

The second quotation is a fact because it can be proved. The number of people with cystic fibrosis in the United States could be confirmed by checking medical records.

The first quotation is an opinion. The first two words of the quotation ("I think...") tell you very clearly that the statement is the writer's personal belief. Another person could have a different belief, for example: "I think that the motivation of animal-rights activists is to demonstrate their respect for all forms of life."

A writer can support an opinion with facts, or with other opinions. Facts help to strengthen an argument. Which of the arguments below do you find more convincing?

opinion
|
• Suspect X should be charged with the theft because he was riding the stolen bike.

|
supporting fact

opinion
|
• Suspect X should be charged with the theft because he looks suspicious.
|
another opinion

How to Tell an Opinion From a Fact

If you think that a statement is a fact but you're not sure, ask yourself these questions.
• Is there a way of checking this statement to see if it's true?
• Could this statement be confirmed by looking in a reference book?
• Could I prove this statement by measuring or counting something?
• Would most people agree with this statement?

If you answer yes, you are probably looking at a fact. If you answer no, you are probably looking at an opinion.

More About Facts and Opinions

It is not always easy to tell the difference between a fact and an opinion. Sometimes facts and opinions even sit beside each other in the same sentence. Look at the sample paragraph on the next page, taken from the opinion piece on pages 84–86. Some sentences have been numbered for clarity.

A fact is a statement that can be proved true. A statement that is proved false isn't a fact —it's either a lie or an error. Consider the statement "The earth is flat." It definitely looks like a fact, but your knowledge of geography tells you right away that the statement is false and therefore isn't a fact.

What happens when you don't have enough knowledge to decide whether a statement is true or false? Take another look at this fact: "There are only about 10,000 people with CF in the United States." Without researching it, very few readers will be able to say whether that claim is correct. Probably the writer is telling the truth. But it is possible that the writer has made an error or is deliberately lying.

When you read an opinion piece (or any kind of writing that claims to tell the truth), it is important to remember that *statements that look like facts aren't necessarily true.* Use a reliable source, such as an encyclopedia or a dictionary, to help you decide whether a statement is true. And since every source has a bias, it's even better to check more than one source.

How has research using animals helped those with CF? (1) Three times a day my daughter uses enzymes from the pancreas of pigs to digest her food. She takes antibiotics tested on rats before they are tried on humans. (2) As an adult, she will probably develop diabetes and need insulin—a drug developed by research on dogs and rabbits. If she ever needs a heart-lung transplant, one might be possible because of the cows that surgeons practiced on. There is no animal model to help CF research, but once the CF gene is located, new gene-splicing techniques may create a family of mice afflicted with the disease. (3) Researchers would first learn to cure the mice with drugs, then cautiously try with humans.

(1) Fact. It is possible to verify each detail in the first sentence. For example, it would be easy to check whether Claire gets three doses of enzymes every day.

(2) The second part of this sentence is a fact that could be verified. But the first part of the sentence is an opinion. Words such as *probably, possibly, may,* and *might* indicate some degree of uncertainty. Claire might not develop diabetes and she might not need insulin. More facts would be useful.

(3) Opinion. Words such as *would, should,* and *could* are signals for opinions. Opinions also often contain words that make a judgment, such as *good, bad, better, inferior, intelligent, clumsy, boldly,* and *cautiously.*

Identifying Facts and Opinions

Now it's time for you to test your knowledge of facts and opinions. Read the sentences below, identifying each one as a fact or an opinion. Some sentences might be part fact and part opinion. With each identification, include a brief explanation that tells how you reached your decision. Where possible, your explanations should refer to specific words in the sentences.

1. "My daughter has cystic fibrosis."

2. "Finally a hospital test of the salt content in her sweat led to the diagnosis of cystic fibrosis."

3. " 'Your daughter will not have a long life, but for most of the time, it will be a good life.' "

4. "We moved to California where the winters aren't so harsh and the cold and flu season isn't so severe."

5. "Researchers should be thanked, not hassled."

6. "We can still hope—as long as the research continues."

You can use a chart like the one on the next page to organize your work.

Once you have completed your chart, use the checklist below to assess your work. Then compare your ideas with the answers printed at the bottom of this page.

Sentence	Fact or Opinion	Explanation
My daughter has cystic fibrosis.	*F*	*I could check this by finding out about the author and her daughter. Would be difficult though. Most readers won't know.*

CHECKLIST: FACTS AND OPINIONS

 Did I identify each sentence as a fact, an opinion, or a combination?

Did I explain my decision?

Did I identify words that suggest doubt or that make a judgment?

 Are there any apparent facts that would be hard to check? Could they be exaggerations, errors, or lies?

Did I identify a way to check the apparent facts?

The Art of Persuasion

LEARNING EXPECTATION

○ You will analyze the arguments in "Do We Need to Use Animals in Research?" by identifying specific persuasive techniques.

○ You will then assess the effectiveness of the opinion piece.

Approach #1: "Let's go to the movie. It's got your favourite actors, and every review I've read says their performances are great. Besides, tickets are half price today."

Approach #2: "Come on; you're my best friend. The movie will be no fun without you. It's stupid to stay home and do nothing. Don't be so cheap."

Understanding the Task

The writer of a piece of persuasive writing is trying to influence your thinking. But you probably don't want to be told what to think. You want to make up your own mind. That means you will have to decide for yourself if you agree with the writer's arguments. Is the writer giving you proof you can rely on? Or is the writer trying to slip something past you?

You can learn the standard techniques writers use to make their arguments persuasive.

Getting Ready

As you read the following pages, you'll see which persuasive techniques carry the most weight. At the end, you'll be asked to assess the arguments in an opinion piece.

Logic Versus Emotion

Here are two ways you might try to persuade a friend to go with you to the movies.

The first approach uses logic to develop a rational argument. It builds its case around facts, and around opinions easily supported by facts or observation. The second approach relies on an appeal to emotion. It tries to make the friend feel guilty for not going. Rational argument and appeal to emotion are the basic techniques of persuasive writing. Sometimes a writer uses one technique more than the other, but most writers use both techniques at the same time to improve their chances of persuading the reader to agree with them.

Appeal to Emotion

People don't always think about issues logically. They often make decisions based on their emotions. Writers can take advantage of this habit. In the first paragraph of her opinion piece, Jane McCabe makes several attempts to arouse your feelings.

1. **The Personal Connection** In the second sentence of the first paragraph on page 84, McCabe addresses you as an individual: "If you had to choose…." It's as if she were talking with you personally, almost as a friend.

She wants you to identify with people who depend on medical research. She tells you her daughter's name (paragraph 1) and talks about Claire's life (paragraphs 2–4) to make you emotionally involved in the issue.

2. **Dialogue With the Reader** The first paragraph on page 84 also includes two questions readers are meant to answer in their heads. McCabe uses these **rhetorical questions** to set up a dialogue with you. A good writer can phrase a rhetorical question so that most readers will automatically think of the answer the writer wants.

3. **Loaded Words** A loaded word is one that triggers an emotional response. McCabe's second sentence contains good examples. When she describes her "cute, blond, brown-eyed daughter," she creates a picture of a person you can care about. Without the loaded words, the sentence doesn't have the same impact: "If you had to choose between saving a dog or a human, whose life would you choose?"

The Rational Argument

It isn't wrong or unfair to appeal to the reader's emotions when building an argument. In fact, it would be foolish for a writer to ignore such a powerful technique. But an appeal to emotion doesn't prove anything.

A reader might respond, "I want to agree, but I need some solid evidence before I can accept your point of view." That's why most opinion pieces include rational arguments.

1. **Providing Reasons** To be persuasive, a writer must support his or her opinion with strong reasons. McCabe starts this process in her first paragraph.

> **Opinion**: Animals should be used in research.

> **Reason**: Research offers the only hope for a cure for cystic fibrosis.

In paragraph 5, McCabe supports the idea that research is vital. She gives five pieces of evidence to support her claim that animal testing has already helped people with CF. Strong arguments are based on facts. Notice that McCabe includes several facts in paragraph 5. Take a moment to list them.

2. **Counterattack** Another way of building a rational argument is to state an opposing argument and then show its weakness. McCabe uses this technique in paragraph 8.

> **Opposing argument**: "There are advocates for animals who only seek to cut down on 'unnecessary research.' "

> **Counterattack**: "They don't specify how to decide what is unnecessary…."

Assessing an Opinion Piece

Now, assess whether or not "Do We Need to Use Animals in Research?" is a convincing opinion piece. Follow these steps.

1. Write down your first impression of the piece. Do you agree with McCabe?
2. Make your own copies of the two charts shown here. For each of the techniques on the left-hand side, find as many specific examples from the opinion piece as you can. You may include examples that are mentioned in this Tutorial and in Tutorial 11. One example is already given.
3. Look at your charts to see if McCabe relies more on appeal to emotion or on rational argument. Do you think McCabe has built a strong case for her point of view? Do you still agree with your first impression of McCabe's argument?

Once you have completed the two charts, team up with a classmate who is also working on this Tutorial. Use the checklist below to assess your and your classmate's work. Identify any differences in your charts, and discuss why they are different.

Appeal to Emotion

Technique	Example
Personal Connection	• "If you had to choose...." (paragraph 1, sentence 2) •
Dialogue With the Reader	• •
Loaded Words	• •

Rational Argument

Technique	Example

Reasons:
    Opinions
    Facts
	•
	•
	•

Counterattack:	• •

CHECKLIST: THE ART OF PERSUASION

✓ Did I find examples of each of the five persuasive techniques mentioned in the Tutorial?

✓ Did I identify by paragraph and sentence number where I found each example?

✓ Did I identify whether McCabe relied more on appeal to emotion or on rational argument?

✓ For the topic of the opinion piece, do I think appeal to emotion or rational argument is the more persuasive approach? Why?

✓ Did I support my conclusion with examples from my charts?

✓ Did I find any weaknesses in McCabe's argument? If so, what are they?

Reading Consumer Information

LEARNING EXPECTATIONS
In this section, you will learn
- to recognize the purpose of consumer information
- to identify two common types of consumer information
- to recognize and use different ways of organizing information
- how to analyze advertisements

What Is Consumer Information?

Consumer information is produced to inform people about products that are available and to encourage people to buy. The most obvious kind of consumer information is advertising. Every day you are surrounded by it—in newspapers and magazines, on TV and radio, and on billboards, subway posters, and clothing. Advertising promotes products but offers very little information.

Consumer articles are much more subtle than advertisements in their overall messages. They invite you to think before you buy a product. But the message may still be "You want something—go out and buy it." Some articles give general advice about what to look for when buying a product, such as a bicycle or a car. Others compare different brands of the same product and recommend

the best buy. A consumer article in *Consumer Reports* may even encourage you not to buy a product, while other articles, such as one about bicycles in a fitness magazine, may have a strong bias towards encouraging a purchase.

Advertisements and consumer articles both use similar persuasive techniques. They may
- give only some of the facts
- link a product to an attractive lifestyle
- claim to be on "your" side
- appeal to your emotions
- support claims with "expert" opinions

 (See pages 105 and 106 for other persuasive techniques.)

The Elements of Consumer Information

Here are the main elements found in most consumer information, with some tips on how to identify them.

1. Product Image Consumer information is designed to create an image or a personality for a product that will appeal to the consumer's emotions. When you look at an ad or a consumer article, ask yourself
- How does it make me feel?
- How is the product made appealing to the consumer?

2. Art Photographs or drawings are often the most important element of consumer information. Bright or unconventional and unexpected images are often used to grab the viewer's attention. Most consumer information is created using bright colours, but black-and-white art is sometimes used to create a particular "look." Many ads feature a **logo** or symbol associated with the product. As you look at the art in consumer information, ask yourself

- Why were these particular images chosen for this product?
- What do they say about the product?

3. Copy All the words that appear in an ad or an article are the copy. Usually there is a snappy **headline** in bold type. Study how the article or ad is organized into sections to make the information easy to read. Notice how bold type draws your eye to different parts of the ad or article. There may also be a **slogan** associated with the product. As you read the copy, ask yourself

- How is the copy designed to appeal to the consumer?

4. Target Audience Consumer information is designed to appeal to specific target audiences. For example, jeans ads often target teenage shoppers. The age, gender, interests, social class, income, and values of the target audience are all considered when consumer information is designed and written. To identify the target audience, ask yourself

- What is being said about the product and the kind of person who will use it?
- What are the interests and values being appealed to by the art and the copy?

How to Read Consumer Information

The main thing to keep in mind when reading consumer information is that someone may be trying to sell you something. Don't let yourself be talked into buying something you don't need or want.

Be clear about your own purpose when you read or view consumer information. If you do want to buy something and are gathering information, be skeptical. Ask yourself: How dependable is this information? Might this writer have a bias? For example, fashion magazines are full of advertisements for beauty products. Do you think articles in these magazines are likely to be critical of their advertiser's products?

A consumer article about buying bicycles appears on pages 96-101 and an ad for a bicycle appears on page 106. Before you read them both, make a list of questions you would want answered if you were going to buy a bicycle. Read both items once, ignoring the notes in the margin of the article. Identify each of the elements of consumer information, and make notes. How many of your questions have been answered? Do you have any new questions about the bicycles, the article, or the ad?

Then read the article and ad again, this time including the notes in the margin of the article. How do these notes compare with your own? When you've read them twice, work through the Tutorials on pages 102 and 105.

reading

1 The title gets right to the point. But do I really need a "perfect" bike?

2 The article is about choosing the best style and getting the right fit for a bike.

HOW TO BUY

From choosing the best style to getting the right fit, here's all you need to know

KATHRYN KUKULA

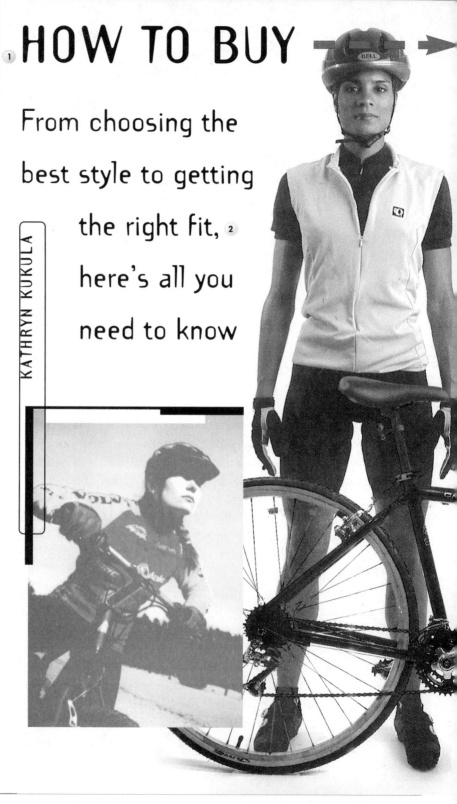

THE PERFECT BIKE

The Bike For You

Buying a bike these days can be an intimidating experience. With thousands of models to choose from, how do you find the one that's best for you? Start by picking the right type of bike. Answer these questions and you can't go wrong.

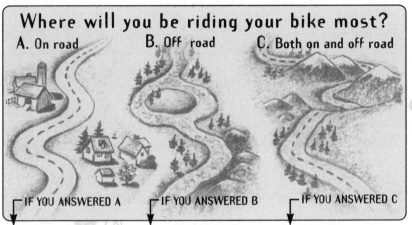

Where will you be riding your bike most?

A. On road   B. Off road   C. Both on and off road

IF YOU ANSWERED A   IF YOU ANSWERED B   IF YOU ANSWERED C

3 This diagram is easy to read. I use a bike for getting around my neighbourhood.

How will you be riding on road?

1. Fast, competitive riding such as a triathlon.
Buy a: **Road Racing Bike**
2. Riding for fitness over medium distances — 16–64 km.
Buy a: **Sport Touring Bike**
3. Long distances — over 64 km a day — and perhaps camping overnight.
Buy a: **Touring Bike**
4. Leisurely rides around your neighborhood — 16 km maximum per day.
Buy a: **Sport Touring or Hybrid Bike**

Where will you be riding off road?

1. On dirt roads, grass trails or smooth, packed dirt trails.
Buy a: **Hybrid or Mountain Bike**
2. On steep, rugged trails with rocks, roots and other obstacles.
Buy a: **Mountain Bike**
3. On a combination of smooth and rugged terrain.
Buy a: **Mountain Bike**

How will you be riding on and off road?

1. Short distances on pavement to get to off-road trails.
Buy a: **Mountain Bike**
2. I'll transport my bike to off-road trails, but I also want to ride on paved roads in my neighborhood.
Buy a: **Hybrid* or Mountain Bike ****
3. Over 16 km at a time on the road; off-road riding on smooth, packed dirt trails.
Buy a: **Hybrid Bike**

*If you're riding on smooth, packed trails
**If you're riding on rugged trails

4 These are five types of bikes. Are these really all the types available? This article is aimed at serious bikers.

❹ The FIVE Basic Bikes

Sport Touring ·········

Not quite as delicate as a racing bike but much more responsive and speedy than a regular touring bike, a sport touring bike has 18–21 gears to help you over steeper hills, and drop handlebars that allow for varied hand positions and excellent downhill control. If you want to regularly go for rides of more than 16 km and challenge yourself to some fast pedaling, this aerodynamic bike is definitely for you.

Touring ·········

A touring bike is a comfortable workhorse for distance riding. Drop handlebars provide good control on downhills and allow for a variety of hand positions, which helps prevent fatigue and neck pain on long rides. You'll find attachment points for fenders, racks and saddlebags for camping gear. Twenty-one gears will get you over any mountain; cantilever brakes can stop a heavy load. These bikes are not built for speed, but for comfort over the long haul.

Mountain ·········

Mountain bikes have sturdy frames, straight handlebars and fat, knobby tires on wheels that are slightly smaller than road-bike wheels. The upright riding position and fat tires make these tough bikes comfortable to ride. Straight handlebars give you extra leverage on steep inclines, and a strong frame and various bike components will withstand rough, off-road riding. Keep in mind that on the road it takes a lot of energy to push this bike's heavier frame and knobby tires.

Hybrid 5

The hybrid looks like a thinner, taller mountain bike: straight handlebars, medium-width tires on road-bike-size wheels. For riding short distances, running errands or commuting, this bike is perfect. The upright riding position makes it easy to see traffic and scenery. It's lighter than a mountain bike, and more comfortable but not as fast as a road bike. Twenty-one gears will help you go anywhere. However, on long rides your arms may tire using straight handlebars, and it's not durable enough for rugged trail riding.

Road Racing

These superthin, ultralight bikes are built for speed. Their short wheelbase — the distance from axle to axle — makes them respond to the slightest movement. Aerodynamic additions such as aerobars (narrow, forward-pointing handlebars) and composite wheels (three-to-five-spoked wheels) take minutes off your time, and the 12 or 18 gears are just enough to get you up to top speed and keep you there. You'll want these features for winning races, but not for comfortable, relaxed recreational riding.

5 What does "hybrid" mean?

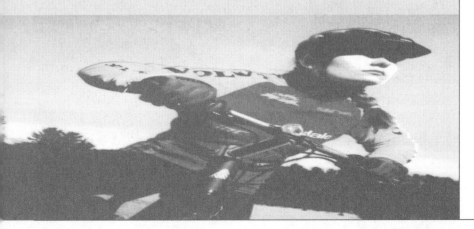

Getting the RIGHT Fit

The next step is choosing a bike that really fits your body, allowing you to ride comfortably and efficiently.

There are two ways to find the right bike size. The more precise method is to pay a good bike shop $50 or so to fit you to a bike using a standardized computer program called The Fit Kit. They'll measure the length of your legs, torso and arms and come up with a frame height and length (the distance from the seat post to the handlebars) that's best for your body.

Check frame height You can also choose a bike by trying out different models at a bike shop. First, check the frame height by straddling the bike. Pull aside bikes that have 2.5-5 cm of clearance between the top tube and your crotch, three to four inches if you're going to be riding on rough trails. Pick bikes from different manufacturers, as they all design frames differently.

Compare frame length Among the bikes you've pulled aside, note the differences in frame length. Most bikes are designed for men's shorter legs and longer torsos, so even if you can stand over the bike easily, the handlebars may be too far away when you're on the seat.

Take a test ride Most important, ride the bikes to see which feels best. You should feel comfortable and in control. Your elbows should be relaxed and slightly bent, and you should be able to move around easily on the bike with your feet on the pedals—slide your butt back so it hangs off the saddle, move your hands to various positions on the handlebars, and flex and round your back.

Adjust seat and handlebars Most important is the seat height: Your knee should have a 25- to 30-degree bend when the ball of your foot is on the pedal at its lowest position. Then, adjust the handlebars so they're 2.5 cm lower than, or the same height as, the seat. If you need to change the bike's length slightly, put on a shorter or longer stem—the part that holds the handlebars to the frame. If you have trouble grabbing the brakes, the bike shop can adjust the brakes or order you handlebars designed for women. You can also try straight bars instead of drops, or different styles of straight bars, which have varying degrees of upward curve.

6 Fifty dollars to fit a bike is expensive! Is this writer promoting The Fit Kit?

The Comfort Guide

If you're sore during or after a ride, chances are your bike needs adjustment. Here's advice from Matt Pulisic, a physical therapist in Richmond, Virginia, on how to fine-tune bike parts to prevent pain. **7**

Aching knees: Raise your seat. Too much knee bend puts stress on the joint. Or slide the saddle back to reduce knee bend. Check your position: The front of your knee should be directly over the center of the pedal when the pedal is halfway up. Try loosening your toe clips so your lower leg can rotate slightly with each stroke.

Sore neck: Raise your handlebars. Low handlebars require you to look up all the time, overextending your neck. Also, ride with your elbows slightly bent, not locked, to ease neck strain.

Sore lower back: Put on a taller stem to raise the handlebars. Or try to put a curve in your back when you ride: Tilt your saddle forward to allow your pelvis to rotate forward slightly, to get a natural concave curve in your lumbar spine. **8**

Numb fingers: Change your hand position. Too much bend in your wrist compresses the nerves, causing pain and numbness. Move your hands around on the handlebars during a ride and try to keep your wrists straight. If you have straight handlebars, consider purchasing bar ends to allow for more hand positions.

Sore bottom: Make sure your saddle is level—it should be 2.5 cm higher than handlebars—and wide enough at the back so you are sitting on the bones of your pelvis under your butt. Saddles with wide noses may cause inner-thigh chafing. Try a narrow-nose saddle or wear snug cycling shorts.

7 Advice from a physical therapist. How do I know he's really an expert?

8 I like the way the information is organized. The layout makes it easy to understand.

How much do the bikes cost? Which is the best brand? Where could I find out about that? I wonder where I could get a good second-hand bike?

How Consumer Articles Are Organized

Understanding the Task

The purpose of the article "How to Buy the Perfect Bike" is to sell bicycles in general, not one specific brand of bicycle. The writer provides information that appeals to readers of the magazine, who are interested in fitness and may have money to spend.

The writer of the consumer article has used several frequently used patterns of organization that make the article easy to read.

Getting Ready

Here are six ways to organize information.

1. Describing Each of the sections under the heading "The Five Basic Bikes" **describes** one kind of bike—the kind of riding it's designed for, and its handlebars, brakes, gears, appearance, and special features.

You could lay out the information in a web, with the topic in the centre and the impor-tant details around it. Making a web like this helps in preparing to write a description.

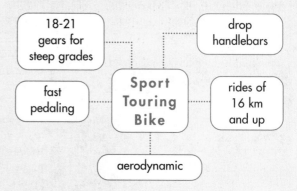

Make a diagram of the information in the paragraph about the road racing bike.

2. Main Idea and Supporting Details One kind of description begins with a sentence about a main idea, and then adds details, examples, or explanations. The touring bike paragraph is organized this way.

Main Idea	Supporting Details
A touring bike is a comfortable workhorse for distance riding.	• drop handlebars: good control • variety of hand positions • • •

Complete the chart by adding three more details from the paragraph.

3. Comparing and Contrasting Sometimes articles examine the similarities and differences between things. Words that signal similarities are *also, besides, as well, in addition.* Words that signal differences are *however, but, although, instead, on the other hand.*

In the article, the hybrid bike is compared to the mountain and road racing bikes. Take notes about the hybrid and mountain bikes using a diagram like the one below. The similarities are listed where the circles overlap so they stand out.

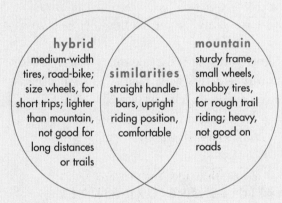

With a partner, make a similar diagram to compare the hybrid and road racing bikes.

4. Problem and Solution "The Comfort Guide" on page 101 of the article uses a problem-and-solution pattern of organization. Words like *since, because, result in, therefore,* and *so* signal the use of this pattern. Each box in "The Comfort Guide" tells you about one physical problem related to bike riding and offers solutions.

You could take notes for the information about "Sore neck" in a chart like this.

Problem	Solution
sore neck	1. raise handlebars to avoid overextending neck 2. ride with elbows slightly bent, not locked

Set up a chart like the one above, and add information from two other boxes in "The Comfort Guide."

5. Listing Words like *first, second, next, then, after, before, also,* and *in addition* signal the use of a list. The section "Getting the Right Fit" uses a list. The signal is in the first sentence in the second paragraph: "There are two ways to find the right bike size."

The words "two ways" tell you that this is a list containing two items. Find the signal words in these sentences.

- "You can also choose a bike by trying out different models at a bike shop."
- "First, check the frame height by straddling the bike."

The list can be laid out this way.

> **Getting the right fit in a bike**
>
> 1. Use a computer program at a bike shop.
> 2. Try out different models at a bike shop.
>   a. check frame height
>   b. compare frame lengths
>   c.
>   d.

Fill in the rest of the list above. Use the bold-face headings in the article to help you.

6. Cause-and-Effect The section "The Comfort Guide" can be summarized this way.

Cause	Effect
poorly fitted or adjusted bike	→ *aching knees* → *numb fingers* → *sore neck* → *sore lower back* → *sore bottom*

This is an example of a cause-and-effect pattern of organization. One cause, a poorly fitted bike, leads to many uncomfortable effects on the rider.

With a partner, create a diagram to show the possible effects caused by these situations:
- broken brake cables on a bike
- not finishing a race

Using Patterns of Organization

Choose a consumer product you know well —shampoo, in-line skates, jeans, running shoes, or anything you find interesting. Working alone or with a partner, brainstorm a list of features that would be discussed in a consumer article about the product you have chosen.

Then use one or more patterns of organization to make a plan or an outline for a consumer article about your chosen product. Prepare charts and diagrams like the ones demonstrated in this Tutorial to show how you would organize the article. If signal words are part of a pattern of organization you are using, include some in your plan.

Show your plan to a classmate who has also completed this activity. Assess each other's work using the checklist below.

CHECKLIST: HOW CONSUMER ARTICLES ARE ORGANIZED

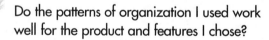 Do the patterns of organization I used work well for the product and features I chose?

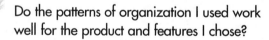 Do my charts or diagrams clearly demonstrate the patterns of organization I used?

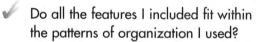 Do all the features I included fit within the patterns of organization I used?

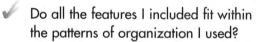 Did I use any signal words to clarify the pattern of organization?

Analyzing an Advertisement

LEARNING EXPECTATION
You will analyze how advertisers use art and copy to sell their products.

Understanding the Task

Every element of an advertisement—the art, the copy, and the layout—is carefully chosen to help sell a product. Here are just a few of the persuasive techniques advertisers use.

- associating a product with an appealing lifestyle and attractive people
- playing on emotions like vanity, the need to belong, or concern for the environment
- bandwagoning (Everybody's doing it; you should too!)
- celebrity endorsements
- recommendations from experts
- humour

Being aware of the techniques that advertisers use will help you to be a more critical consumer.

Getting Ready

When analyzing the message of an advertisement, you should examine the following elements.

1. Advertising Language Words have literal meanings, but they also appeal to our emotions and connect with our previous experiences. Advertisers choose words with positive associations to appeal to their target audiences.

Compare the two sentences below. Which is intended to provide information? Which is intended primarily to sell a product?

- These state-of-the-art biking shorts pamper you with silky-smooth seams and an ultra-soft chamois lining that wicks moisture away from your skin.
- These biking shorts have flat seams and a chamois lining that draws sweat away from the skin.

The first sentence is a selling message full of words with positive associations: *state-of-the-art, pamper, silky-smooth, ultra-soft.*

With a partner, rewrite this sentence using words with positive associations: *This is a fast, sturdy bike.*

Read the copy in the Electra Bicycle advertisement on the next page and list all the words with positive associations. What kind of image do these words create for the Electra Bicycle?

Work with a partner to list words with positive associations for one of the following products.
- breakfast cereal
- jeans
- shampoo

What kind of image do these words create for the product?

2. Target Audience and Art The art chosen for an advertisement usually reflects the age, gender, interests, social class, income, and values of the target audience. Study the art in the Electra Bicycle advertisement and answer the following questions.
- What do the blurred background and wheels of the bicycle suggest?
- Why is the bicycle on an angle?

- What do the clothing and hairstyle of the rider suggest?
- Why is the rider making this gesture?
- Why isn't the rider wearing a helmet?

Describe the target audience for this ad. Are you part of that audience?

3. Copy Copy for advertisements is generally written to create an image for a product, not to give information about it. Make a list of the information you would want to have if you were planning to buy a bicycle. Now look at the Electra ad.
- What information does the ad give about the bicycle?
- How much of the ad is devoted to creating an image for the bicycle and how much to giving information?

Writing About an Ad

Find an ad for a product you would like to have. Write your responses to the ad using the chart below to organize your thoughts.

Decide whether or not you think the ad is effective. With a partner, compare your opinion. Would you make any changes to your chart after working with your partner?

Response to an Ad	
Target Audience Who is the intended target audience: their age, gender, interests, and values?	• • •
Art How is the product made appealing? If models are included, who are they, what do they look like, and what are they doing?	• • • •
Copy What is the purpose of the copy? How does it appeal to the target audience?	• • •
Layout How does the ad catch your attention?	• •
Mood or Impact What overall feeling does the ad create?	• •

CHECKLIST: ANALYZING AN ADVERTISEMENT

✔ Did I examine the advertising language, target audience, art, and copy in the ad?

✔ Did I identify features that appeal to me and features I don't like?

✔ Did I describe the overall mood or impact of the ad, using my own words?

✔ Did I identify any strengths or weaknesses in the ad?

✔ What changes would I recommend to make the ad more effective?

✔ Did I explain how my suggested changes would appeal to the target audience?

Reading Power Tools

P Perhaps the most important reading strategy is choosing a selection that will interest you or that will tell you something you need to know. You can see that each of the characters in this cartoon has chosen to read something of personal interest.

Drawing by W. Miller; © 1987 The New Yorker Magazine, Inc.

General Strategies

The following reading strategies will help you get the most out of reading, whether you're reading for enjoyment or to find information.

YOUR REASON FOR READING

Knowing why you are reading will help you focus more clearly on your task. As a student, your reason for reading is often given in an assignment. When your teacher gives you an assignment, read the instructions carefully. They will help you understand your reason for reading. Look for key words that define the task. Here are some examples.

1. Read pages 93–98 in *Math Basics* — exact resource
   — activity
   for discussion in class on Wednesday.— time restriction

   Reason: to understand the math lesson

2. Prepare a brief class presentation to — amount of detail

   explain how volcanoes are formed.— topic

   Reason: to find enough information to use in a class presentation

3. Write a three-page essay in which you — amount of detail

   — topic
   describe the life cycle of an insect of

   your choice. Due February 17.— time restriction

   Reason: to find enough information to use in an essay

Your reason for reading will help you decide
- how fast to read
- how to prepare for reading
- what to do as you read and afterwards

The Tutorials on pages 25 and 27 offer more detailed information on specific reading tasks.

If you have any questions about a reading assignment, even after reading the instructions carefully, ask your teacher or a classmate for some help.

YOUR TURN

Rewrite the following instructions in your notebook and label the key words. Explain the reason for reading for each assignment, as in the chart on page 109.

1. Write a one-page book report about a novel of your choice.

2. Read the opinion piece on pages 84–86 of your textbook and assess the strength of the writer's argument.

SCANNING

You use scanning techniques when you want to find a specific piece of information in a book or another resource. To scan a page of text, have the word or number you're looking for in mind and let your eyes move quickly across the lines and down the page. Focus only on finding that word or number; don't read for sense. Once you have found the word or number, read the sentences around it to find the information you seek.

Use the index or table of contents to find which pages to scan for specific information. For example, if you are doing research on insulin and the index of a book lists a reference on page 142, turn to that page. Then scan for the word "insulin" and read the surrounding sentences. Scanning reading material can save you time when you are doing research or looking up specific facts.

YOUR TURN

Turn to the newspaper article "9.84," starting on page 72, and scan for the name "Namibia." Find the name of the runner representing that country in the 100-metre race. For further practice in scanning, choose a textbook you are currently using and scan for specific information related to a class assignment. Use the index and table of contents to choose which pages to scan.

SKIMMING

When you skim something, you look it over quickly to get a sense of its contents. Skimming has two main purposes.
1. to help you decide whether a book or article contains information you need
2. to prepare for in-depth reading
Skimming can save you time when you are doing research.

To skim a book, you look at the title, cover illustration, any notes or summaries on the book jacket, and the table of contents. You might flip through the book to see how the contents are laid out and what kind of visuals it contains.

To skim a chapter in a book or an article, you look at the title or headline, and any headings, introductions, or summaries provided. You also look at the visuals and their captions. You may also read the first sentence of several paragraphs, or the first and last paragraphs.

Skim a section of this book that you have not yet read, and describe briefly what it is about. Or, if you are doing a research project, find two or three books on your topic and skim them to decide if you should read any of them more closely.

READING RESPONSE JOURNAL

TECHNOLOGY TIP

Keeping a journal on a computer is easy. You don't have to worry about leaving enough space for later entries, because the computer will always allow you to insert additional text.

For a Double Entry Journal (see page 113), you can set up a two-column chart or table that will allow you to keep related entries side by side, even if one entry is much longer or shorter than the other.

A Reading Response Journal is your opportunity to write in a relaxed way about the selections you read. You can ask questions, give your opinions, make comparisons with other things you've read, and express your ideas in words or drawings and diagrams.

For more on using a Response Journal while reading fiction, see the Tutorial on page 25.

Responding is also an important part of reading non-fiction. Here are some questions you can use to help spark your response to different types of non-fiction.

- For a news article: Has anything like that happened around here?
- For an opinion piece: Do I know anyone who thinks like this? How does this argument make me feel?
- For a news article or a how-to book: Could I do this myself?
- For consumer information or an opinion piece: Why do I feel manipulated?

Here are two types of journal entries you might try while reading either fiction or non-fiction.

Reacting	Reflecting
Why can't Pauline just get used to her new horse? She's being silly.	I've never had a pet, but my best friend said she could never imagine replacing her pet cat. I didn't realize how attached people can be to animals. I guess Pauline isn't really so silly.

Bebe: The writer really makes Bailey sound like a hero for winning that race. Was it such a big deal?

Christel: I think almost everyone in Canada stopped what they were doing to watch the race, or listen to it on radio. I'll always remember seeing Bailey do his victory lap with the Canadian flag. It was a big deal at the time.

Double Entry Journal

Divide your journal page into two columns labelled Reacting and Reflecting. In the Reacting column, write your first thoughts, feelings, and questions about the selection, and any quotations you find interesting. In the Reflecting column, respond to what you wrote in the first column after rereading the piece and discussing it with others.

Dialogue Journal

In a dialogue journal, you communicate back and forth with another person—a reading partner, your teacher, your parents, someone on the Internet—about what you are reading. You can also create an imaginary dialogue between you and a character in a book or a favourite author. You write both sets of entries, but for one set you adopt the role of another person.

YOUR TURN

Use one of the types of journal entries described above as you complete your next reading assignment. Then discuss with a classmate or reading partner how keeping the journal improved your understanding or appreciation of the selection you read.

TONE

The attitude that a writer has towards a subject influences the way he or she writes about it. Authors express their attitudes in the **tone** of their writing. Authors create tone through the words and the details they include in their writing. For example, an author might write about the Internet using any of the following tones.

- A straightforward tone: Here's how to get the information you need on the Internet.
- An irritated tone: How can anyone possibly weed through all the junk on the Internet!?!
- An outraged tone: I found a lot of stuff on the Internet that I wouldn't want my seven-year-old to see!
- A nostalgic tone: I'm glad I spent my youth in a great library filled with beautiful books instead of surfing the Net.
- A humorous tone: Help! I lost my mind in cyberspace!

Other tones a writer might use include the following: critical, emotional, serious, reflective, sarcastic, sad, joyful, provocative, exaggerated, respectful, and ironic.

YOUR TURN

Get a daily newspaper and turn to the opinion page or to the page with the editorials and the letters to the editor. Read two or three selections and identify the tone of each. Share your selections with a classmate and see if your classmate agrees with the tone you have identified.

RECOGNIZING BIAS

A **bias** is a tendency to see a subject only one way and to ignore other ways of looking at it. Biased writing tries to give you a shove towards seeing the subject the way the author does. Here are four questions you can ask to help you recognize bias.

1. What is the author's background? Try to find out if the author has a reason for taking a particular side. For example, if you are reading an essay entitled "Saving Our Forests," written by an employee of a logging company, you should be on the lookout for a bias in favour of continued logging.

COMPARING BIAS

Sometimes you can see bias more clearly when you compare two or more pieces of writing that cover the same topic. Doing a comparison will make you more aware that writers actively choose which details to present. For a detailed look at this technique, see the Tutorial on page 78.

2. Does the writing present more than one side of the story? Look to see whether different points of view are expressed and whether they are treated equally. In biased writing, one point of view may be stressed, and others omitted or misrepresented.

3. Does the writing contain loaded words? A loaded word triggers an emotional response. Look at how the loaded words in the following two sentences create two very different impressions of the 15 people who stayed in the village.

- A group of 15 freedom fighters rested in the village.

- The village was occupied by a gang of 15 terrorists.

4. Does the writing contain stereotypes? A stereotype is a very simple and often prejudiced view of someone or something. Age, gender, race or ethnic group, appearance, poverty, and wealth are the basis for many stereotypes. For example, older people may be stereotyped as weak and out of touch with today's issues. But many older people are strong and well informed. Every person should be considered as an individual.

TECHNOLOGY TIP

Be careful when you notice stereotypes that appear in print or on the Internet. When stereotypes are included, it's a sign that the information may be biased.

YOUR TURN

Skim one section of a daily newspaper until you find a story you think may be biased. Read the story closely and answer the four questions above. Discuss your conclusions with a classmate and see if he or she agrees with you. If the story is biased, how would it change if told from a different bias or from a less biased point of view?

SYNTHESIS

To **synthesize** information means to take several pieces of information and shape them into a meaningful whole. For example, imagine you are creating a classroom report about breakthroughs in law enforcement. You read several newspaper and magazine articles to find information about your topic. You use synthesis when you put the information together and show how it relates to your topic. See the example below.

Newspaper Article	Magazine Article	Synthesis
A national computer network is being developed so police across the country can share information.	DNA evidence helps police solve crimes.	Police are drawing on the latest technology to track down criminals.

You may also have to use synthesis to understand how the different parts of a textbook, a news article, or another selection relate to each other. Synthesis is a creative process because you are combining information in new ways to fit your own ideas or expand your understanding.

YOUR TURN

Read two or three reviews of a movie you've seen or two or three articles about your favourite sports team. Use synthesis to combine information from the reviews or articles. Then write one paragraph expressing your own opinion about the movie or the team and create a chart like the one above to demonstrate the synthesis.

FORMING CONCLUSIONS

When you form a conclusion, you review the information or evidence you've read and make up your own mind about it.

Here are four steps that you can follow when you want to form a conclusion.

1. Briefly state your goal.
2. Decide on at least three or four factors that are important.
3. Use the important factors to organize your information.
4. Reach your conclusion by **analyzing** the evidence. To analyze something, you break it down into its parts and look at each part closely. Organizing information in a chart can make analysis much easier to do.

1. *I want to buy a bike.*

2. *The most important factors for me are price, how the bike rides on off-road trails, how reliable the bike is, and how it looks.*

3.

	Bike #1	Bike #2	Bike #3
Price:	*$360.00*	*$310.00*	*$499.00*
Good for off-road:	*rugged but heavy*	*rugged*	*rugged and very light*
Reliability:	*ok*	*great*	*ok*
How it looks:	*ugly*	*very ugly*	*great*

4. *Bike #3 looks great and is very light, but it's more than I can afford to pay. Bike #2 is the ugliest, but it's the most reliable. If I spend the extra $50 and get Bike #1, I get a less reliable bike that's still ugly. I think I'll buy Bike #2.*

YOUR TURN

Think of a decision you will have to make, such as what kind of summer job to look for or what courses to take next year. Use the four steps described above to form a conclusion.

Reading for Appreciation and Enjoyment

 The following reading strategies will help you get the most out of reading fiction and non-fiction for appreciation and enjoyment.

POINT OF VIEW

The point of view identifies the person telling the story. The chart below shows the three kinds of point of view that you'll meet most often in stories and novels.

Point of View	Story Text	Who's Telling the Story
first-person	"I was getting fed up with saying goodbye. One month five kids disappeared from my shrinking class at Copelin High School." — from "The Visitor" by Christine Pinsent-Johnson	a story character
third-person limited	Willy felt like he was spending his whole life saying goodbye. It seemed like every other day one more person left his class at Copelin High School. — adapted from "The Visitor"	a narrator who knows the thoughts of only one story character
third-person omniscient	Copelin was a dying community. Moving vans and red-and-white U-Haul trailers were a weekly sight on its pot-holed streets. — adapted from "The Visitor"	a narrator who knows everything

When you read a story or novel, identify the point of view the author has chosen and think about these questions.

1. Why did the author use this point of view to tell the story?
2. Would you have used the same point of view?
3. How does the person telling the story influence your thoughts and feelings about the characters and events?
4. How would the story change if it were told from a different point of view?

YOUR TURN

Choose a favourite story and rewrite one event from the point of view of another character. Share your rewrite with a partner. Or, for a novel you have read recently, try to answer the four questions above. With a classmate who has read the same novel, talk about your answers. Does your classmate agree with your answers? If not, why not?

PREDICTING

Before you read a story, you make guesses or predictions about what will happen based on the title and what you know of the author. You continue to make predictions about what will happen next and how the story will end. You should base your predictions on

- what you already know about the characters
- what has already happened in the story
- what you know about people from your own experience
- the plots of other stories you have read

You can also make predictions when you're reading non-fiction. For example, after reading the opening paragraph of an opinion piece, you can try to predict the arguments the writer will use to support his or her opinion.

YOUR TURN

Try this activity, called Reading Like a Writer. It shows a way to read a story using predictions.

- Form a small group of three or four and choose a story to read.
- Have each member of your group fold a piece of paper into four equal sections and number each section.
- Divide the story into four sections.
- Have everyone in the group read the first section of the story silently or have one member read the section aloud to the group.
- In the first section of the piece of paper, have each member of the group write the answer to this question: "If you were the writer, what would you have happen next?"
- Share and discuss your responses with your group. Be prepared to support your ideas with details from the story.
- Go on to read the next three sections in the same way, making predictions and discussing the rest of the story.

When you've finished reading the story, write in your Response Journal about this experience. Did you enjoy reading the story this way? How did it help you understand and appreciate the story?

SETTING

The time and location in which a story takes place is called the **setting.** In some stories the setting is very important, but in other stories it is hardly mentioned. As you read a story or novel, ask yourself these questions about the setting.

1. What does the author tell you about the place where the story happens? Are the weather, the time of year, the landscape, the buildings, and the historical period described?

2. Are the characters in conflict with the setting? For example, must a character survive a storm or escape from a burning building? Is the setting an obstacle to any of the characters?

3. What does the setting tell you about the characters? What does it reveal about how much money the characters have, their position in society, or their emotional state? Does the setting influence the way you feel about the characters?

4. How does the setting contribute to the atmosphere or mood of the story? Is it bright and cheerful or dark and frightening? How would you describe it?

YOUR TURN

Think of a novel, story, or drama you have read recently, and answer the above questions about the setting. Share your answers with a classmate who has read the same selection. Does your classmate agree with your answers? If not, why not?

CHARACTERS

The following questions help you to identify and get to know the main characters in a story.

- Who are the main characters in the story? Who are the minor characters?
- Which of the characters do you identify with most?
- Do any of the characters remind you of people you know? If so, explain why.
- Is the story told from the point of view of one or more of the characters? If so, name them.
- What events are the characters involved in? Which is the most important event?

- Do any of the characters' actions surprise you? If so, explain why.
- Does the story focus on conflict among the characters? Is any one character involved in more conflicts than the others? If so, which one?

YOUR TURN

After reading a short story, novel, or drama, jot down the answers to the above questions and discuss them with a classmate who has read the same selection. You might create a character web to organize your thoughts about the characters (see page 54). Together, decide which actors should play the part of each character. Use quotations from the selection to support your choices.

CONFLICT

Conflict is the basis of every story. Conflict occurs when characters experience problems. We keep reading because we want to find out how the problems will be solved. Conflict can be serious, or light-hearted and humorous.

There are two basic kinds of conflict in literature: **external conflict** and **internal conflict**.

External conflict is the struggle between a character and something outside of him or her. That something could be
- Nature: the weather, the landscape, or animals
- People: family, friends, or strangers
- Situations: war, poverty, unemployment

Internal conflict is a struggle that takes place within a person. This struggle usually involves making choices
- between good and evil
- between self-interest and helping others

If you are analyzing the conflict in a story, novel, or drama, you could use a chart like the following to organize your thoughts.

Type of Conflict	What Happens	Solution to the Conflict
•	•	•
•	•	•

YOUR TURN

Create a chart like the one above and use it to analyze the conflict in one of the selections in this book or in another selection of your choice. If you have trouble filling in the chart, start by simply listing what happens in the story in the second column, one main event at a time. Then fill in the third column and leave the first column till last.

SYMBOL

A **symbol** is an object, an animal, or a person that suggests something else, such as an idea or a belief. For example, a crown is the symbol for a monarch, a dove is a symbol for peace, and a police officer is a symbol of law and order. Writers often use objects, people, or animals in a symbolic way. For instance, a writer might use a tiny green shoot of grass growing in a ravaged landscape as a symbol of hope and rebirth.

Recognizing symbols will help you understand the literature you read. Symbols are usually
- visual
- repeated several times
- related to the theme of the selection

In the story "The Visitor," the burned-out theatre on Main Street is a symbol of the loss of hope in the town of Copelin.

Choose a story, novel, poem, or drama you have read and create a symbol map for it. Choose one symbol for each section (chapter, stanza, set of paragraphs) of the selection, and choose at least two quotations to support your choice. Discuss your choices with a classmate who has read the same selection. You could use a chart like the following to organize your ideas.

Section or Page Reference	Symbol	Supporting Quotations
1st section, pages 15 & 16	empty houses	"He...spent his days running after people for overdue rent and closing up empty houses." "Out of a dozen homes on the street five were empty."

READING A NOVEL

A novel is like a short story, only much longer and more complex. A short story may include only a few characters, but a novel may include dozens. The action in a short story usually covers a short span of time and a few locations, but novels can cover many years and many locations. Here are a few tips for reading a novel.

- If you are allowed to choose your own novel, take the time to find one that you'll really enjoy. Ask friends or librarians for recommendations. Skim the novel to get a feel for the plot and writer's style before you settle on a choice (see page 111).

- Set a realistic schedule for reading the novel, and don't let yourself get behind.
- Keep a Reading Response Journal (see page 112), and use some of the following Reading Power Tools to help you remember and understand what you read.

- If possible, create a reading discussion group with classmates who are reading the same novel. Meet regularly, at least after every few chapters, to discuss your thoughts and questions.

YOUR TURN

If you are currently reading a novel, use one of the Reading Power Tools listed above to help you remember and understand the characters and events. If you are not reading a novel, go to the library and use your skimming skills to choose a novel you think you will enjoy.

CREATIVE RESPONSES TO LITERATURE

Responding creatively to a story, novel, poem, or drama helps you to become personally involved with the characters, the events, and the author. You can examine your own ideas about the work and how it relates to your own life and values.

Here are some ideas for creative responses to literature.

1. **Change the point of view**. Rewrite a story from the point of view of another character to explore that character's thoughts and feelings.

2. **Continue the story**. Use your imagination to tell what happens to the characters after the story ends or to add a stanza to a poem. Imitate the writer's style.

3. **Write a diary entry**. Express the private thoughts and feelings of one of the characters in the story.

4. Express your opinion. Tell what you think about a character's behaviour and how you might have acted differently.

5. Retell it in a different form. Retell the story as a news story, a radio or TV script, or a fable or folk tale, or in a form of your choice.

6. Present the work in a visual form. Make an illustration, a comic strip, a poster, a collage, a video, or a diorama to express something about the selection.

As you work on your creative response, remember to keep your work true to what happened in the original selection. For example, if you are rewriting the story from the point of view of one character, you need to know exactly what that character experienced in the story.

YOUR TURN

Choose one of the ideas described above and use it to respond to a story, novel, poem, or drama of your choice. Share your work with a partner or a small group.

Reading for Information

The following reading strategies will help you locate, gather, and organize information.

USING THE LIBRARY

The best place to start looking for information is a library. In a library, you'll find
- reference works
- periodicals
- books
- non-print resources
- computer networks

Before you begin to read any resource, set a specific goal for your reading and use scanning and skimming techniques to help you find the information you need. Avoid wasting time reading through long books or searching through complex CD-ROMs that hold little useful information. The charts on pages 128–130 tell you a little about the different resources you will find in a library.

YOUR TURN

Choose a research topic: it could be a topic you have been assigned, or one you find interesting. Then, look over the resources listed in the charts on pages 128–130. Which resources do you think would be most useful for your topic? Be prepared to explain your choices.

Resources

1. Reference Works

Types	Dictionaries	Encyclopedias	Atlases	Indexes
Best Uses	→ brief definitions of words and phrases	→ general information about many subjects	→ maps and other geographical information	→ lists of information available in other resources
Shortcuts	→ A key or set of instructions at the front of the reference work usually tells you how to use it. → Many reference works are organized in alphabetical order. → Check for guide words at the top of each page.			
How to Find Them	→ Look in the reference section of the library for general reference works. → Ask the librarian for specialized reference works, such as biographical dictionaries, encyclopedias of science, and so on.			

2. Periodicals

Types	Newspapers	Magazines
Best Uses	→ current events and issues → up-to-date information about sports, entertainment, fashion, and so on	→ detailed and up-to-date coverage of current events, sports, fashion, and so on → good colour photographs
Shortcuts	→ Look for a brief table of contents on the front page, and separate sections for news, business, sports, entertainment, and so on.	→ Look for a detailed table of contents near the front. → Look for magazines on specific subjects, such as sports, music, fashion, and so on.
	→ For both, skim headlines, photos, graphics, captions, first paragraphs, boxed material, and subheadings to find specific information.	
How to Find Them	→ Libraries have current issues of newspapers and magazines. → Older issues might be stored on microfilm or microfiche. → Use a news or periodical index to find specific articles quickly.	

3. Books

Types	how-to books, biographies, histories, textbooks, and so on
Best Uses	→ detailed information about specific topics → extensive information on broad subject areas → time-tested information from past and present experts
Shortcuts	→ Check the cover for a summary of the book and the author's qualifications. → Check the date of publication to see how current the book is. → Use the table of contents at the front of the book and the index at the back to help you find the information you need. → An introduction or a preface may explain the book's purpose and structure.
How to Find Them	→ Use the library's catalogue to search for books by author, title, or subject. → When you find a useful book, look at the books near it on the shelf. They might also be helpful. → Other useful books may be listed in bibliographies at the back of books and end of articles.

4. Non-Print Resources

Types	CD-ROMs, software, videos, photographs, art collections, and so on
Best Uses	→ allows you to see your subject, such as what a historical period looked like, or how a science experiment was done → quick sources of specific information and visual materials (charts, graphs, photographs) → can be used to add interest to presentations and displays
Shortcuts	→ Read or skim any overviews or guides that accompany a non-print resource. → Check the copyright date to find out how current the resource is. → Keep detailed notes about where you find information so that you can find it again quickly. → For CD-ROMs and software, read the main menu carefully and return to it often. Learn how to use the "help" and "search" functions. → Find out how to copy or print information from the resources you choose.
How to Find Them	→ Ask a librarian to help you locate non-print resources. → Some resources, such as videos and CD-ROMs, may be listed in special catalogues.

5. Computer Networks

What they are	The Internet, the World Wide Web, Schoolnet, and so on. **Warning**: Be critical of information found in these resources. Check for bias and stereotypes, and make sure any facts mentioned can be verified by reliable sources.
Best uses	→ specific information from known sources, such as a government department → specific information from an expert, using e-mail → unverified information and opinions from bulletin boards
Shortcuts	→ Take any Internet training offered by your school, or ask a friend for help. → Ask clear questions so you get the information you need. → Use any "help" and "search" features available. → Keep track of where you have been on the Net, so you can return to the address later. → Find out how to download and/or print information from the Net. → Some Web sites contain unreliable information. Ask a teacher or librarian whether the information is reliable. → Don't count on these resources for all your information—it may be faster to use other resources.
How to find them	→ There may be a few computers in your library with access to the Internet. Ask the librarian. → Use a search engine to identify information sources for specific topics.

PREPARING TO READ

This is a good time to remind yourself of your reason for reading (see page 109). Then choose one of the following strategies to help you get the most from your reading.

1. Preview and Predict Use your skimming skills to preview the resource, and then make some predictions about the information you'll find. This should help you choose which material to read more closely. Or use the SQ3R strategy, explained on page 133.

Title of Article or Chapter	Prediction
The Future of Recycling	This article will be about new recycling methods.
Urban Canada	This chapter will be about Canadian cities.

2. **What You Already Know** Brainstorm a list of what you already know about your topic. You could use the KWL strategy, explained below.

YOUR TURN

Choose a resource that you have not yet read, such as a news article or a chapter in a textbook. Use one of the strategies described above to help you prepare to read. Then read the resource. How did your preparation help you to get more from your reading?

THE KWL CHART

The KWL chart is one way to get information from a resource.
- **K** stands for what I already KNOW.
- **W** stands for what do I WANT to know.
- **L** stands for what I have LEARNED.

Organize your KWL chart in three columns: one for K, one for W, and one for L. You will fill in the K and W columns before you start to read, and the L column during or after your reading.

In the K column, list everything you already know about your research topic. Thinking about what you already know can help you to focus more clearly on what you need to find out next.

In the W column, list questions about your topic. These questions will give you specific goals for your reading. Look at the headings in the resource to help you think of questions. For example, the heading "The KWL Chart" might lead to questions like these: What is a KWL chart? What do the letters KWL stand for?

Fill in the L column as you read or after you have finished reading. Jot down the answers to your questions and any other information you think is important.

How to Buy the Perfect Bike		
K	W	L
I know you can buy racing bikes and mountain bikes. Mountain bikes are heavier and have fatter tires.	What other kinds of bikes are there? How are they different from each other?	There are sport touring, touring, mountain, hybrid, and road racing bikes.

YOUR TURN

Work with a small group and use the KWL chart to guide your reading of a chapter from a textbook or an information article from a magazine. Compare your group's chart with that of another group that has read the same resource. Discuss any differences in your charts and see if the other group can answer any questions you still have.

There are five steps in the **SQ3R** reading strategy: **S**urvey, **Q**uestion, **R**ead, **R**ecite, and **R**eview. This strategy is most useful when you are reading a textbook or studying for a test.

1. Survey This step is like skimming. Read titles, headings, and subheadings. Look at any visuals and read the captions. Look for words in special type. Read the first and last paragraphs of sections or chapters, looking for main ideas. Do this step quickly to get a general idea of what you'll be reading. Surveying the material will make it easier to understand later.

2. Question In this step, you generate questions to help focus your reading. This is similar to the second step of KWL. Your survey of the material can help you think of questions. For example, you can turn headings, key words, or topic sentences into questions.

Headings	Possible Question
Preparing to Read SQ3R	How can I prepare to read? What is SQ3R?

Read the selection in small sections. Think of a new question for each new heading or key word. If there are no headings, divide the selection into sections of a few paragraphs each.

3. Read Read to find the answers to your questions. Read carefully and take enough time to understand the material. If you can't answer a question, read the material again, pausing to think about each sentence. If you still can't answer the question, try rephrasing your question.

4. Recite Demonstrate that you understand what you have read by explaining it in your own words. You can explain it out loud, either to yourself or to a partner. Or you can explain it in writing. Do the Recite step each time you finish reading a section.

SUCCESS TIP

Do you want to achieve success on assignments and tests? Research has shown that the Recite and Review steps will help you remember what you've read.

5. Review Within 24 hours of reading the material, review what you have learned. If you haven't taken notes so far, do so now. You'll find more information on note-taking in the Tutorial on page 64. If you did the Recite step in writing, you can look over the notes you made then. You should review your notes one more time immediately before a test.

YOUR TURN

Choose a challenging section of a resource book to read. Use the SQ3R strategy to read the section. Then in your journal or with a partner, consider whether the strategy helped you understand the material you read.

IDENTIFYING MAIN IDEAS

A **main idea** is like a thesis in an essay. It identifies the topic and tells the reader something important about that topic. All of the other sentences or paragraphs in the selection add details to support the main idea.

Topic	Main Idea
Buying bicycles	It can be difficult to choose which bicycle to buy, because there are many different models available.
The Juno Awards	The Juno Awards are annual awards given by the Canadian Academy of Recording Arts and Sciences (CARAS) in honour of the best of the Canadian music industry. (*The Canadian Encyclopedia, 2nd ed.*)

But how do you recognize a main idea? Sometimes it is stated clearly in a topic sentence at the beginning or end of a selection. The main idea of a textbook chapter is usually identified by the chapter title, section headings, and highlighted key terms. But in some kinds of writing, the main idea may be implied rather than clearly stated.

To identify an implied main idea, follow these steps.

1. Identify the topic of the paragraph or selection. What is it about?
2. Jot down or highlight each supporting detail.
3. Synthesize the details into a single sentence. That single sentence should identify the main idea. (See page 116 for more on synthesis.)

To be sure you have identified the main idea, test it with these questions.

- Does every sentence in the paragraph or selection say something about the main idea you have identified?
- Are all of the details clearly related to the main idea you have identified?

If you answered yes to both of these questions, you have identified the main idea. If not, you need to review the details and revise your sentence.

YOUR TURN

Read the following paragraph and use the three steps described above to identify the main idea. Then, with a classmate, use the questions to test your main idea. Did you both identify the same main idea? Discuss any differences.

Some people love dogs and others adore cats. Dog lovers appreciate the loyalty, affection, and protectiveness that so many dogs seem to display. Those who love cats admire the way cats refuse to compromise. They like cats for their boldness, their sense of privacy, and their independence. But there are other people who don't like cats or dogs—they prefer snakes.

What Do Good Writers Do?

You've been given a writing assignment, and now you're desperately wondering what the first sentence should be. If you're stuck in front of a blank page or screen, you may be trying to do too much at once. Writing is a process. It helps if you break down your task into small steps. Below are the steps in the writing process, as well as some suggested activities for each step. You can choose the activity that would be most useful for your writing task.

1. Pre-Writing

- Start by planning. Ask yourself
  - What do I want to say?
  - Who will my readers be?
  - How do I want my readers to respond to my writing?
- Brainstorm on your own or with others.
- Discuss your ideas with classmates, friends, family.
- Gather information from books, the media, experts, and your own experience.
- Write well-organized notes about the information you find.
- Choose a form (e.g., poem, memoir, essay, speech).
- Create an outline or a plan.

2. Drafting

At this stage, make your first attempt to express your ideas.

- Don't worry about being perfect; just write what comes to mind.
- Double-space your writing so there's room for notes and changes.
- Follow your plan, but be willing to try new ideas.
- Write notes on your draft about different ideas and approaches to try.
- If you're really stuck, move on to another section. You can always come back later and try again.

3. Revising

In this step, think carefully about how you can improve your writing. You may repeat this step more than once for some pieces of writing.

- If possible, put your draft away for a day. Then read it with fresh eyes, asking your-self these questions.
  - Does it make sense?
  - Is my meaning clear?
  - Do I have any questions about what I have written?
  - What do I like or dislike about my writing?
- Read your draft from your readers' point of view so you can make changes to suit their needs.
- Read your work aloud to check whether it sounds right to your ear.
- Get another person to read your draft, looking for strengths and weaknesses.
- Make big changes if necessary—cutting, adding new material, and moving sections around.
- Prepare a new draft with all the changes you've decided to make.

4. Proofreading

Use this step to correct and polish your writing.

- Read your work several times, looking for errors in grammar, spelling, punctuation, word choice, and so on. Look for a different kind of error each time you read.
- Use dictionaries and writing handbooks to double-check your corrections.
- Read your writing aloud again, making small changes to improve the flow.
- Ask someone to help you proofread your work.

5. Publishing

Now that you've finished writing your selection, it is ready for its audience. You can use word processors, computer graphics, special paper, and your own art to make your finished writing eye-catching and enjoyable to read.

Different Kinds of Writing, Different Approaches

The writing process is not a set of rules; it's a set of possibilities. You won't go through the same steps in the same order every time you write. You'll have to decide what's the best approach for each piece of writing you do. Here are some examples of the different approaches for different kinds of writing.

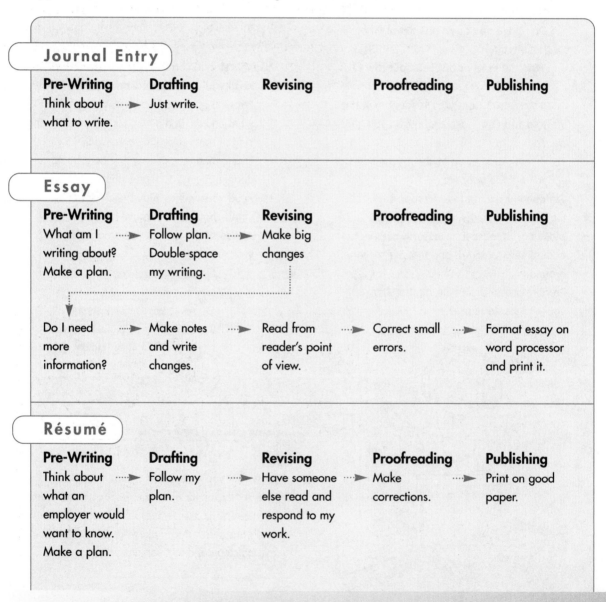

Journal Entry

Pre-Writing	Drafting	Revising	Proofreading	Publishing
Think about what to write.	Just write.			

Essay

Pre-Writing	Drafting	Revising	Proofreading	Publishing
What am I writing about? Make a plan.	Follow plan. Double-space my writing.	Make big changes		
Do I need more information?	Make notes and write changes.	Read from reader's point of view.	Correct small errors.	Format essay on word processor and print it.

Résumé

Pre-Writing	Drafting	Revising	Proofreading	Publishing
Think about what an employer would want to know. Make a plan.	Follow my plan.	Have someone else read and respond to my work.	Make corrections.	Print on good paper.

Writing About Ideas and Information

An inspiring idea may help you begin a writing assignment. But where do you start if you aren't hit with inspiration? And how do you make sure you communicate your ideas so your readers will understand and appreciate what you have to say? As a writer, you must decide who will read your writing, what you want to say, and how to make your writing interesting so it will hold your readers' attention. This unit offers strategies aimed at helping you write effective paragraphs, essays, science reports, and job applications, even if you aren't inspired.

PEANUTS reprinted by permission of United Features Syndicate, Inc.

Writing Paragraphs

LEARNING EXPECTATIONS
In this unit, you will learn
- about the structure of a paragraph
- how to use a plan to help you write a paragraph
- how to identify the form and purpose of a paragraph

What Is a Paragraph?

A paragraph is a group of sentences written about one main idea or topic. The main idea is often expressed in a topic sentence. You start a new paragraph when you introduce a new idea, a new point of view, or a new speaker.

The Elements of a Paragraph

Every paragraph is unique. There are many ways to organize a paragraph, depending on your purpose and your topic or main idea. But every paragraph you write should have the following three elements.

1. **The Topic Sentence** clearly identifies the main idea in a paragraph. It tells the reader what the paragraph is about. A topic sentence frequently appears near the beginning of a paragraph, although it need not be the first sentence. Sometimes the main idea of a paragraph is implied rather than stated outright in a topic sentence. But unless you're writing a story, it is a good idea to include a topic sentence in every paragraph you write.

2. **Supporting Sentences**, sometimes called the body, give more details about the main idea of the paragraph. The details should be presented in an order that is easy to follow. The details may be facts, examples, reasons, or added description.

3. **The Closing Sentence** makes it clear that the paragraph is finished. A closing sentence sometimes restates the main idea of the paragraph. A closing sentence may also challenge the reader with a question, deliver a strong final detail or example, or provide a link to the main idea of the next paragraph.

The Structure of a Paragraph

The structure of a paragraph should demonstrate **unity**, **order**, and **coherence**.

Unity means that a paragraph has one main idea. It describes one thing or one experience, or explains one idea or one opinion. All of the supporting sentences in your paragraph develop or expand on the one main idea. In the paragraph below, notice how each supporting sentence gives more details about each step in the water cycle.

Order means that the details in a paragraph are organized in a way that makes sense. Here are three ways to think about organizing the details in a paragraph.

1. **Logical Order** organizes the details so one idea leads logically to the next, for example, least important to most important, general to specific, familiar to new or unknown.
2. **Space Order** puts the details in an order relating to the physical world, for example, left to right, top to bottom, close to far away.
3. **Time Order** puts the details in an order relating to time (hours, days, months, and so on), for example, past to present, present to future, first to last.

Coherence means that all the ideas in a paragraph flow naturally from one to another. You can make the flow of ideas easy to follow by using linking or transition words, such as *first, second, finally, then, now, to the left, to the right, before, later* (see page 147).

Notice the unity, order, and coherence of the paragraph below. It explains the steps in the water cycle. The details are arranged in time order, and the linking words used are *as soon as, at once, later.*

On pages 142 and 143, there are two sample paragraphs written by students. Identify the topic sentence (or implied topic), supporting sentences, and concluding sentence of each paragraph. What changes might you suggest to the writers to improve the unity, coherence, and order of these paragraphs? The notes in the margins might help you.

Topic Sentence —— **As soon as** precipitation reaches the surface, it starts making its way back up into the atmosphere. Some of it evaporates directly from the land and water surface. Plants begin **at once** to use any water that reaches them. **Later** they give off vast amounts of moisture into the atmosphere through a process called transpiration. The moisture released by evaporation and transpiration forms clouds. The clouds **later** return the moisture to earth, completing the water cycle.

Supporting Sentences

Concluding Sentence

Descriptive Paragraph

—from a short story called "Snow Flake," written by Ivanka Koulik, a student at Martingrove Collegiate.

Outside, the girl, dressed in clothes that had not been washed in weeks, with tears everywhere and half-hearted mendings ① here and there, looked at her reflection in the glass. "Oh, my gosh!" she exclaimed. "Look at my hair," she thought. She raised her dirty, bony hands and combed her fingers through ② her hair, remembering the once beautiful brown hair with waves that her father said reminded him of calm waves in the ocean. Her fingers did not get very far, for they got caught in ③ one of the numerous rat's nests of knots she had. In the glass she could see her hair, ends poking out everywhere. "So dirty," she thought. Catching a glimpse of her pale face, a tear dropped onto her cheek. Her attention was soon diverted to the woman sitting inside. Plump, with rosy cheeks, clean, ④ fashionable clothes, with her hair tied back, she looked forty or forty-five. A look of horror and disgust was smeared on ⑤ her face; however, what drew the girl's attention was the meal on the table. "M-m-m! Food!" thought the girl and instinctively her stomach grumbled. She hadn't eaten in a while and the food bank had nothing left to give out. ⑥

1 This sentence is really long. Had to read it twice. Not a topic sentence.

2 I can almost see how dirty and thin she must be.

3 The knots are in her hair?

4 We've moved inside.

5 This part here seems a bit confusing.

6 I guess the paragraph is about the contrast between the street girl and the rich woman.

Opinion/Persuasive Paragraph

—from an essay written by Stephanie Soo,
a student at Martingrove Collegiate, about the novel
Who Has Seen the Wind, by W. O. Mitchell.

Mr. Digby, principal of the town's school, demonstrates the compassion in human behaviour. Mr. Digby is sensitive to others and realizes the harshness of the Young Ben's life. He understands that "the boy's father; the drunken, irresponsible and utterly mindless Ben…[is] completely unaware of the demands of family or community," (p. 73)* forcing the Young Ben to grow up with no guidance. He is also an intelligent person who uses his knowledge of Plato, Aristotle, and the Utilitarian and Stoic viewpoints to explain ideas to others like Milt Palmer. Mr. Digby is also extremely generous, as he offers to pay the Wongs' grocery bill and for the rifle the Young Ben stole. Similarly, he is also moral, as he refuses to give in to Mr. Powelly's intentions of sending the Young Ben to reform school, risking his job in the process. Finally, Mr. Digby is empathetic because he perceives that if you "get [a] child to talk without frightening it out of him," (p. 71)* you will gain his respect rather than his resentment. Undoubtedly, Mr. Digby is a very sympathetic, patient, and open-minded person whose caring nature illustrates man's capacity for compassion.

*The page references are to the novel *Who Has Seen the Wind*.

1 This is what the paragraph is about.

2 Good use of quotation.

3 Describes Mr. D.'s behaviour in general.

4 More examples of Mr. D's actions.

5 Must be the last point in the paragraph.

6 Empathetic?? Look this up.

7 Repeats topic of paragraph. Hey, what about woman's capacity for compassion?

Writing a Paragraph

LEARNING EXPECTATION

○ You will plan and write a paragraph that develops one main idea.

Understanding the Task

Planning a paragraph can make writing it easier. Like planning the route for a trip, planning a paragraph can help you avoid getting lost and wasting time.

Getting Ready

Every paragraph has a main idea, a topic sentence, supporting details, and a concluding sentence. The steps of this Tutorial should make it easier to write a paragraph with all of these elements.

1. **Topic or Main Idea** It may be as short as a single word or as long as a sentence. If you need more than one sentence to describe your main idea, you need to narrow it down. Here are three ways to generate ideas for writing.

- **Brainstorming** Work with a partner or a small group and write down every topic idea you can think of in three minutes. Work quickly. Accept every idea, no matter how strange. Go wild!

- **Word Association** On a blank piece of paper, write down a word related to an activity or issue that interests you. Then build a web of words related to your first word, and expand the web as far as you can on one page. Then look over your web and choose a few related words and rephrase them as a sentence. This could be your writing topic.

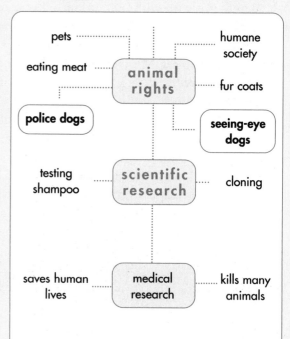

Sentence: The same rules should be used in caring for all working animals, whether they are used for scientific research, or as guide dogs or police dogs.

- **Recent Experiences** Make a list of experiences you have had recently. Think of movies, parties, friends, books, music, sports, family, school, and work. Choose one experience and write about it.

2. **Type of Paragraph** Once you have a topic for your paragraph, you must decide what type of paragraph to write. Look at the chart on page 147. Choose the type of paragraph that suits your topic and your purpose for writing.

3. **Topic Sentence** A topic sentence should identify your main idea and say something about it. Look at the main ideas and topic sentences in the chart below.

4. **Supporting Details** These can be developed in point form. List as many details as you can, and then cross out the weak ones and any that are off topic.

5. **Concluding Sentence** This sentence should provide a strong conclusion or climax to your paragraph. Writing it as you plan gives you a clear ending to aim for.

What follows is a plan that the writer might have used to prepare for writing the paragraph on page 143. Notice that the order of ideas changed from the plans to the finished paragraphs. Changes such as these are a natural part of the writing process.

Outline for an Opinion/Persuasive Paragraph
Main Idea: Mr. Digby is a kind and compassionate man.
Topic Sentence: Mr. Digby demonstrates compassion in his behaviour.
Supporting Details:
- sees how difficult Young Ben's life is (quotation, p. 73 from the novel)
- helps Young Ben by offering to pay for the stolen rifle
- uses his education to help others, like Milt Palmer
- offers to pay for the Wongs' groceries
- resists Mr. Powelly's plan to put Young Ben in reform school
- understands young people (quotation, p. 71 from the novel)
Concluding Sentence: Mr. Digby is a very sympathetic and patient person who shows compassion for others.

Main Idea	+ Your Thoughts	= Topic Sentence
medical research on animals	+ helps people with cystic fibrosis	= How has research using animals helped those with CF?
touring bikes	+ comfortable for long rides	= A touring bike is a comfortable workhorse for long-distance riding.
Mr. Digby, a character in *Who Has Seen the Wind*	+ he helped a lot of people in the novel	= Mr. Digby demonstrates compassion in human behaviour.

Preparing Your Paragraph

Follow the steps described in this Tutorial to create the outline for a paragraph. Use the examples as models for your plan.

When you are satisfied with your outline, write a complete paragraph. Allow yourself the freedom to rearrange and revise your ideas as you write, but never lose track of your main idea.

When you have written your paragraph, use the following checklist to assess your writing. You may wish to ask a classmate to read over your paragraph and assess it using the checklist.

CHECKLIST: WRITING A PARAGRAPH

✓ Did I choose the best type of paragraph for my topic?

✓ Is the main idea of my paragraph clear? Do I have a topic sentence?

✓ Do all the supporting sentences focus on the main idea?

✓ Are my ideas in an order that makes sense?

✓ Did I use linking words to show how my ideas relate to each other?

✓ Do I have a strong concluding sentence?

✓ Did I check for errors in spelling, grammar, and punctuation?

Types of Paragraphs

There are different types of paragraphs. The main idea and purpose of your paragraph will help you to decide what type of paragraph you want to write. And the type of paragraph will help you to decide how to organize your information.

Purpose for Writing	Writing Tips	Linking Words

Descriptive
• to describe a person, place, or thing
• to create a clear, vivid picture with words
	Descriptive
	• Organize your details in space order (see page 141).
	• Give sensory details: sight, sound, smell, taste, and touch.
		Descriptive
		   space-order words: *above, below, across, beside, under, next to, inside, opposite, there, outside, around, among, in front of, on top of, over*
		   order-of-importance words: *first, last, most, better, best, least, most important, above all*

Narrative • to tell the story of an event or a personal experience • to tell a short story	**Narrative** • Organize your information in time order (see page 141). • Use personal details to enhance the story.	**Narrative** **time-order words:** *as soon as, at once, later, before, then, after, when, first, second, during, finally, today, yesterday, immediately, soon, next*

Comparing/Contrasting
• to compare two things by telling how they are similar, how they are different, or both
	Comparing/Contrasting
	• Choose several similarities or differences to compare.
	• Compare one feature at a time.
	• Use logical or space order (see page 141).
		Comparing/Contrasting
		   comparison words: *also, besides, as well, again, in addition, also, likewise, similarly, both*
		   contrast words: *however, but, although, instead, whereas, yet, nevertheless*

Opinion/Persuasive
• to state an opinion and provide evidence to support it
• to persuade your audience to accept your point of view
	Opinion/Persuasive
	• State your opinion clearly first.
	• Support your opinion with reasons and concrete examples presented in logical order.
	• Give information to back up your ideas.
	• Acknowledge other points of view but defend your opinion.
		Opinion/Persuasive
		   emphasis words: *again, in fact, truly, for this reason, most important, finally*
		   clarifying words: *for example, that is, for instance, such as, like*
		   summarizing words: *finally, in conclusion, therefore, as a result*

Cause-and-Effect
• to explain the cause-and-effect relationship among events
• to show how a cause leads to a number of effects
	Cause-and-Effect
	• Show how the causes and effects are related.
	• Use time order to emphasize what happened first and what followed.
	• Explain why things happened as they did.
		Cause-and-Effect
		   time-order words (see above)
		   cause-and-effect words: *because, therefore, on account of, for this reason, as a result, consequently, so*

Explanatory/Instructive
• to explain the steps in a process or give instructions
	Explanatory/Instructive
	• State your topic clearly.
	• Explain the process step by step.
	• Use examples or illustrations where appropriate.
		Explanatory/Instructive
		   time-order words (see above)
		   words to add information: *and, also, again, in addition, next, finally, as well, furthermore*

Writing About Reading

LEARNING EXPECTATION
○ You will write a paragraph about something you have read.

Understanding the Task

When you are asked to compare (contrast) two selections, listen for the key words in the instructions. Here are some possible key words and what they mean.

- If you are asked to **explain** a selection, use your own words to tell **what the selection is about**, or what happens in it.
- If you are asked to **describe** someone or something from a selection, give **details from the selection to create a clear picture** of whatever you are describing.
- If you are asked to **compare** two selections, tell how the selections are **alike and different**.
- If you are asked to **summarize** a selection, **briefly identify the main points** and show how they relate to each other.
- If you are asked to **illustrate** something about a selection, **use examples from the selection** to show how something was done or how something works.
- If you are asked to assess a selection, **describe the positive and negative qualities of the selection**, and draw a conclusion.

- If you are asked to **discuss** a selection, use some of the techniques described above to **examine the selection and express your own opinion**.
- If you are asked to **analyze** a selection, **identify and examine the parts or elements** of each selection and **draw a conclusion**.

Getting Ready

Once you understand your task, the next step is to make notes and organize your ideas.

- Read over any notes you made while reading the selection or during class discussions and think about your personal response to the selection.
- Reread or skim the selection to remind yourself of the content.
- Take notes as you skim the selection. Look for quotations or examples that will help with your writing task and include them in your notes (see page 64).
- Use a web, chart, or diagram to organize your notes. If you are describing a character, you could create a character web (see page 54). If you are comparing two poems, you could use a chart to compare elements (see chart on next page).
- Write a tentative title to identify the focus of your writing.

Things to Compare	"Trombone Solo"	"Foul Shot"
rhyme	every other line ends in a rhyme	no rhyme
rhythm	steady, like rap or jazz music, punchy	1st half of poem has a slow rhythm; 2nd half is faster, like the real action of taking a foul shot

Writing Your Paragraph

Organize your notes into a plan or an outline before you begin writing. Review the Tutorial on page 144. Include in your paragraph

- the title of the selection and the author's name near the beginning
- two or more quotations from the selection to support your main idea
- your personal response to the selection

As you begin to write, follow the plan you prepared and refer to the notes you made earlier. Think about what you want to say and just say it. Don't worry about spelling and grammar as you write your first draft. You'll be correcting your writing later.

Then reread your writing and ask yourself

- Does it make sense?
- Have I left anything out?
- Are all questions answered?
- Is there anything I don't like?
- Have I used the best quotations to support my opinions?
- Are my ideas and examples in the best order?

Revise your writing to improve it, where necessary.

When you are satisfied with your work, proofread it to make sure there are no grammar or spelling errors. Then use the checklist below to assess your work. Don't forget that asking someone else to read and comment on your work is always a good idea.

CHECKLIST: WRITING ABOUT READING

✔ Did I give the title and author of the work in the first sentence or first paragraph?

✔ Did I leave out anything I wanted to say?

✔ Did I stay on topic?

✔ Did I support my ideas with details and quotations from the selection?

✔ Did I include my personal response?

Writing Essays

LEARNING EXPECTATIONS
In this unit, you will learn
○ the elements of a five-paragraph essay
○ how to plan an essay to suit a specific audience and purpose
○ how to use an outline to help you write an essay

What Is an Essay?

An essay is a piece of writing several paragraphs long that shows that a writer has researched a topic and thought about it enough to express a clear opinion on it. An essay is written to appeal to a specific audience, for a specific purpose.

Below are descriptions of five common kinds of essays.

1. Persuasive In a persuasive essay, you try to persuade your reader to agree with your point of view. You state your opinion and support it with evidence, such as facts, examples, quotations from experts, and statistics. (See the Tutorial on page 91.)

2. Personal In a personal essay, you write about an experience that you've had or a subject that interests you. You show how the experience has affected your life or you share your thoughts on the subject.

3. Literary In a literary essay, you write about a story, a novel, a poem, an essay, or a film you have read or seen. You share your personal response to the selection and support your opinion with examples and quotations from the selection.

4. Descriptive In a descriptive essay, you describe a person, a place, a thing, or an experience. You use lots of detail about colours, shapes, smells, tastes, and sounds. You also try to create a mood.

5. Research In a research essay, you present information about a specific topic, such as an event in history, a person's life, or a scientific discovery. Your research may include reading, performing experiments, conducting a survey, or interviewing people. You will probably include quotations and statistics in your essay.

The Elements of an Essay

Although there are many different kinds of essays, there are three features that all essays must have to be effective. They must have a **topic**, an **audience**, and a **purpose**.

1. Topic The topic of an essay is broader and more complex than the main idea of a paragraph. Compare the following essay topics with the main ideas from paragraphs.

Essay Topic	Paragraph Main Idea
• Using animals in medical research helps to save human lives.	• Researchers need to use animals to help develop some medicines.
• The characters in *Who Has Seen the Wind* demonstrate the good and evil sides of humans.	• Mr. Digby's character demonstrates the good side of humans.

2. Audience Try to think of an audience other than your teacher. To whom would you like to say something about your topic? It could be a friend, your parents, the principal of your school, or a politician. Thinking about your audience can help you to choose information to include in your essay. With a real audience in mind, you can include the information they need and avoid wasting time telling them things they already know.

3. Purpose Is your purpose to inform? To persuade? Or to entertain? If you want to inform your audience, you should include information that will be new to them. If you want to entertain your audience, it may be easier to choose a topic they already know a lot about.

The following chart shows how the choice of an audience and the choice of a purpose can affect decisions about what to include in and how to write two different essays on the same topic. Notice also that the three elements—audience, topic, and purpose—all affect each other.

Read the essay on pages 152–154 written by a grade 10 English student. Identify the kind of essay it is and it's topic, audience, and purpose. What suggestions might you offer the writer for improving the essay? The notes in the margins might give you some ideas.

How might you change the essay to appeal to a different audience?

	Essay One	Essay Two
Topic	Physical Fitness	Physical Fitness
Audience	members of a fitness club	everyone at school
Purpose	to entertain (humorous essay in monthly newsletter)	to inform (essay for school paper during Fitness Week)
Decision	Write about the weird habits of people that play different sports.	Write about a variety of sports to show that there are activities to suit everyone.

BRUTUS: A PERFECT MAN IN AN IMPERFECT WORLD

by Madeeha Siddiqi,
a student at Martingrove Collegiate

In the Shakespearean play *Julius Caesar*, the character Brutus (1) is portrayed as a perfect man in an imperfect world. He is honourable and believes that the rest of the human race is honourable as well. These two dominant characteristics of being idealistic and honourable are reflected in his orchard soliloquy, funeral oration, and meeting with the conspirators, although his honour is more clearly defined later on in the play when he gets into an argument with Cassius.

Brutus' idealism is reflected in his soliloquy in Act 2: "It must be by his death: and, for my part,/I know no personal cause to spurn at him" (Act 2, Scene 1, lines 10–11). Brutus says that he (2) really has no personal reason to kill Caesar except for the good of Rome: "not that [I] loved Caesar less but that [I] loved Rome more" (Act 3, Scene 2, lines 22–23). Brutus fears that if Caesar is crowned he will become like "a serpent's egg/Which, hatch'd, would, as his kind grow mischievous…" (Act 2, Scene 1, lines 32–33). Brutus says Caesar is like the little snake which unhatched is harmless, but once the shell cracks and the snake is introduced to the world it will become harmful. When Caesar gets the crown, he will be dangerous like the hatched snake because he is able to do whatever he desires. In other words, Brutus is really assassinat- (3) ing Caesar not for what he is now but for what he might become.

Brutus' idealism and his honour are exhibited later on in the play when the conspirators come to Brutus' house to discuss the (4) slaughtering of Caesar. Cassius suggests that all the men who are

1 The thesis—the essay should convince me that this is true.

2 Is this honour? I wouldn't want to be his friend!

3 Is this reason enough to kill him?

4 His idealism is cruel.

present pledge an oath. Brutus vehemently says no. His reply includes the phrases "No, not an oath" (Act 2, Scene 1, line 114) **5** and "To think that or our cause or our performance/Did need an oath; when every drop of blood/That every Roman bears, and nobly bears,/Is guilty of a several bastardy,/If he do break the smallest particle/Of any promise that hath pass'd from him" (Act 2, Scene 1, lines 135–140).

Brutus thinks there is no need to take an oath because every Roman's blood would prevent him from breaking the smallest part of any promise. He says that all Romans are "guilty of a several bastardy" if they break a promise; therefore there is no way that a Roman will ever break a promise. Brutus also believes **6** all of humanity is honourable, so there will not be any need to take an oath.

During the same night, Cassius suggests that Antony be killed along with Caesar. Brutus refuses once again. He says that **7** Antony "…can do no more than Caesar's arm/When Caesar's head is off" (Act 2, Scene 1, lines 182–183). This again shows Brutus' idealism because he believes that all men are good, including Antony.

In Brutus' funeral oration he displays his honour through his statement "…as I slew my best lover for the good of Rome, I have the same dagger for myself, when it shall please my country to need my death" (Act 3, Scene 2, lines 46–48). This reveals that the only reason he killed his best friend was for the good of his country, and he would kill himself as well if his country needed **8** it. Therefore the task of killing Caesar was not sinful but actually honourable.

Brutus' idealism was also reflected at the funeral when he left Antony by himself to address the crowd. He believed that Antony could be trusted because he was honourable. Yet, Antony proved

5 The essay seems to be addressed to someone who knows the play. I don't.

6 This sounds more like honour and idealism.

7 This sounds more honourable than agreeing to kill Caesar.

8 He's willing to die for his country. That's honourable.

that Brutus was surrounded by bad people and lived in an imperfect world. Antony got the crowd to revolt against the conspirators, even though he had given his word that he would speak only good of Caesar and not blame the conspirators for his death.

9 Antony sounds smarter than Brutus, even if he is not to be trusted.

⑨

Nothing reveals Brutus' honour better than his argument with Cassius near the end of the play. Cassius storms into Brutus' tent and demands to know why Brutus is asking for money. Brutus responds that he needs it to feed and pay his soldiers. Since

10 Why does Cassius have money but Brutus doesn't?
11 Seems there are two points in this paragraph.
12 Cassius sounds corrupt.

⑩ Cassius has money, Brutus thinks that Cassius should be happy to share it with Brutus. But at the same time Brutus criticizes Cassius for having his officer Lucius Pella take bribes as ⑪ ⑫ "protection money" from the Sardians. Brutus would never do this. The quotation below proves his honour.

> …what, shall one of us,
> That struck the foremost man of all this world
> But for supporting robbers, shall we now
> Contaminate our fingers with the base bribes,
> And sell the mighty space of our large honours
> For so much trash as may be grasped thus?
> I had rather be a dog, and bay the moon,
> Than such a Roman. (Act 4, Scene 3, lines 21–28)

13 His honour won't help him feed the army.

⑬ Brutus says that he would just as soon be a dog as the kind of Roman who would accept bribes.

As you can see, in this play Brutus' idealistic and honourable character traits make him a perfect man who lives in an imperfect world. These character traits make him vulnerable to the dark side of human nature. But even manipulators like Antony, and Brutus' so-called best friend, Cassius, have to agree that Brutus was "the noblest Roman of them all" (Act 5, Scene 5, line 68). ⑭

14 Maybe Brutus was noble, but Antony sounds more interesting.

Planning an Essay

LEARNING EXPECTATION

You will choose a topic, an audience, and a purpose for an essay, and then find some information on your topic and write a thesis for an essay.

Understanding the Task

To write a good essay, you must spend time planning and preparing ideas and information. If you try to skip these early steps, you may have trouble when you begin to write.

Getting Ready

Here are five steps you can use to plan an essay.

1. **What is the topic of my essay?**
- If your teacher assigns a very specific essay topic, think about how to give it an original or personal treatment.
   Specific Topic: Comment on imagery in the poem "Foul Shot."
   Personal Treatment: "Foul Shot" reminded me of the time we won the district championships. Maybe I can mention that in my essay.
- If your teacher assigns a broad topic, think about how you can narrow it down. What part of the topic interests you most? What do you already know about the topic?
   Broad Topic: Write an essay about cleaning up the environment.
   Narrowing the Topic: I already know how water quality affects fish in our local lakes. I'll focus on that.
- If you must choose your own topic, turn to the next page for some suggestions on how to generate ideas for writing.

2. **Who is my audience?** It is easier to write for a specific audience, such as a friend or the members of a club. Choose a specific audience and use the following questions to help you decide what information to include in your essay.
- What will interest my audience?
- What does my audience already know about my topic?
- How would I talk to this audience? Would I speak formally or informally? How can I create that same feeling in my writing?

3. **What is the purpose of my essay?** Is your purpose to inform, to entertain, or to persuade your audience of something? As you decide on your purpose, choose the kind of essay that will best suit the purpose. Here are five kinds of essays you can choose from.

- If you want to inform your audience, you could write a **research essay** to present new information, or a **descriptive essay** to describe something unusual.
- If you want to entertain your audience, you might write a **personal essay** to amuse them with a humorous story or to surprise them with an unusual memory. Or you could write a **descriptive essay** to show your audience a beautiful scene or to share an exciting event.
- If you want to persuade your audience, you might use a **persuasive essay** to present your opinion about an issue, or a **literary essay** to share your impressions of a story, novel, film, or play.

4. How will I gather information for my essay? At this stage, you will be making notes to help generate ideas and to record information. You could start a pre-writing folder to collect your notes and ideas. (See the Tutorial on page 64.)

Generating Ideas Here are some tips to help you decide where to look for ideas for your essay, and what kind of information to seek.
- Work with a group or partner to brainstorm ideas about your topic.
- Free write whatever comes into your mind as you think about your topic.
- Talk about your topic with a partner.
- Try to create a clear mental picture of the images in a story or poem, or the actual people, places, and events of something you remember. Try to recall details of colour and shape, sounds, smells, tastes, and textures.

You might organize your ideas in a chart or web. For some essays, this may be all you need to start writing. But for most essays, you will have to do some research.

Research If you need specific information for your essay, you must do some research. Before you start, set a clear purpose for your research. You may be looking for a precise fact to back up your opinion. Or you may need some general background information so you can narrow your topic. Take careful notes as you do your research so the information you find will be easy to use when you start to write.
- Use resources such as books, newspapers, magazines, or the Internet to gather information (see Using the Library, page 127).
- Read your diary or look at family photographs to remember a specific event.
- Talk to your family or friends about what they remember of an event.
- Interview an expert on your topic, such as a science teacher, a local business person, or a friend.

TECHNOLOGY TIP

You may be able to contact experts on a subject using the Internet. Look for a newsgroup that shares information about the subject you are researching. You can do this using Netscape or other newsgroup browsing software.

Topic	+ Opinion	= Thesis
Topic: the use of animals in medical research	+ Opinion: It is necessary because it helps doctors save human lives.	= Thesis: It is necessary to use animals in medical research because it helps doctors save human lives.
Topic: the change in the relationship between Willy and his father in the story "The Visitor"	+ Opinion: Willy understands his dad better by the end of the story	= Thesis: In the short story "The Visitor," Willy learns to understand his father better.

5. What is my thesis? A **thesis** is not the same as a topic. A thesis expresses your opinion about your topic. Your thesis is the basis of the opening paragraph of your essay, and it should be written as a single, complete sentence (see examples above). Make sure you can support the opinion in your thesis with the information you have gathered.

Starting to Plan

Follow the five steps starting on page 155 to plan your next essay. Take the time to generate ideas and do some research before you write your thesis. The more information you have, the better prepared you will be to form an opinion and defend it in your essay.

When you have planned your essay and have a clear thesis, use the following checklist to decide whether it is as good as it can be. You may wish to ask a classmate to read over your plan and use the same checklist.

Tutorial 18 will help you turn your essay plan into a complete essay.

CHECKLIST: PLANNING AN ESSAY

✔ Did I present my topic clearly? Did I need to narrow it down or add a personal perspective?

✔ Did I identify the audience and purpose of my essay?

✔ Did the kind of essay I chose suit my topic, audience, and purpose?

✔ Did I write my thesis statement as a complete sentence?

✔ Did I express an opinion about my topic in my thesis statement?

Writing an Essay

You will prepare an outline for an essay, and write the essay based on your outline.

Understanding the Task

Once you have a plan and a thesis for your essay, you are ready to prepare an outline. A five-paragraph essay shows the basic structure of a formal essay, but the length and number of paragraphs in essays will vary, depending on how much information the writer chooses to include.

Getting Ready

An essay outline should include ideas for the opening paragraph, the body of the essay, and the concluding paragraph.

1. The Opening Paragraph The opening paragraph may be the shortest paragraph in your essay, but it is also the most important one. In the opening paragraph, you
- state your thesis
- set the tone or mood of your essay
- capture the interest of your reader
- briefly introduce main ideas or arguments to support your thesis

Read the first paragraph of the sample essay on Brutus, and identify the thesis and the main ideas or arguments the writer introduces. How might the writer revise this paragraph either to set a different tone or to capture the interest of a different audience?

2. The Body In the body or the middle of an essay, you develop the points or arguments you introduced in your opening paragraph. The body of an essay includes at least one paragraph to develop each point or argument in your opening paragraph. Each paragraph should have
- a topic sentence, stating the main point of that paragraph
- supporting details that explain or expand on the topic sentence
- a closing sentence, which may lead into the next paragraph

The main point or argument in each paragraph should be one piece of information that supports your thesis.

Skim the opinion piece "Do We Need to Use Animals in Research?" on page 84, and create a diagram to show how the main idea of each paragraph relates to the thesis of the essay.

3. The Concluding Paragraph This is your last word on your essay topic. You may
- restate your thesis
- summarize your arguments

- draw a final conclusion about your topic
- suggest any action you wish your reader to take, such as reading a book you have enjoyed or supporting a cause

Which of these four functions of a concluding paragraph does the last paragraph of the Brutus essay serve?

On page 160 is a partial outline for a research essay. It shows a topic sentence, concluding sentence, and supporting details for the first paragraph in the three-paragraph body of the essay. This outline shows only one. If you have a lot of information to include, you may need more than three paragraphs. Use a separate paragraph to develop each main idea or argument.

Creating an Essay Outline

Use the sample essay outline on the next page as a model and prepare an outline for your own essay. When you have completed your outline, read it over and use the checklist at the bottom of this page to decide if you are ready to start writing. You may wish to ask a classmate to read over your outline and answer these same questions.

Writing Your Essay

Follow your outline as you write your essay. Use your thesis statement, topic sentences, and supporting details to develop complete and interesting paragraphs. Allow yourself the freedom to revise and reorder your ideas as you write. But do not abandon your outline. If your outline is not working, go back and revise it before you continue to write your essay.

When you've finished writing your essay, credit the sources of information you have used. These may be books and CD-ROMs, or a neighbour you interviewed.

CHECKLIST: CREATING AN ESSAY OUTLINE

✔ Did I write my thesis as a complete sentence? Did it make my opinion clear?

✔ Did I support my thesis with three or more points or arguments?

✔ Did I need more information to support any of my points or arguments?

✔ Did I write a complete topic sentence for each paragraph?

✔ Did I put the paragraphs in an order that makes sense?

✔ Did I restate my thesis in my concluding paragraph?

Research Essay Outline

Opening Paragraph

Thesis: Amateur sport has a proud history in Canada, and a promising future.

Points to be developed:

1. Amateur sport groups were first organized in 1881.
2. In 1961, the federal government first gave active support to amateur sport organizations.
3. Recent successes in international competition show the benefits of amateur sport organizations for Canadian athletes.

Body of the Essay

Paragraph One:

Topic Sentence: In 1881, the first Canadian athletic group to run sports events was formed in Montreal and was called the Montreal Amateur Athletic Association.[1]

Supporting Details:

1. It was made up of swimming, bicycling, and lacrosse clubs.
2. Three years later it became a national organization called the Canadian Amateur Athletic Union.[2]
3. This group encouraged both team sports and individual sports groups to become members.

Concluding Sentence: The organization became the nucleus for all Canadian sports groups and held meetings regularly in Montreal.

Paragraph Two:

~~~~~~~~~~~~~~~~~~~~~~~~~~~~~~~~
~~~~~~~~~~~~~~~~~~~~~~~~~~~~~~~~

Paragraph Three:

~~~~~~~~~~~~~~~~~~~~~~~~~~~~~~~~
~~~~~~~~~~~~~~~~~~~~~~~~~~~~~~~~

Concluding Paragraph

Summary of points: Canadian amateur athletes have a proud tradition behind them and an excellent support system to work with today. The success of Canadian athletes in international competition shows that the support system works.

Restate thesis: I believe that the success of athletes like Donovan Bailey and Silken Laumann is just the beginning of a bright future for Canadian amateur athletes.

Footnotes

[1] Lorne Sawula, "Sports Organization, Amateur." *Canadian Encyclopedia, 2nd ed.* Vol. 3: 2063.

[2] Sawula, 2063.

TECHNOLOGY TIP

Most word processing programs will format footnotes for you. The program will keep track of how many footnotes are in the document, number them in order, and automatically place them at the bottom of the page where the reference appears.

Crediting Sources

There are two ways to credit the information or quotations in your writing: **footnotes** and a **bibliography** (or list of references). Research essays should include both.

Footnotes go at the bottom of the page on which a quotation or fact is included. See page 160 for an example. Or you can keep the notes within your essay, as in the sample essay on page 152. Use the form your teacher prefers.

A bibliography lists all the sources of information you used while researching an essay or report. You should always use at least two sources. The bibliography appears on a separate page at the end of the essay. Each entry lists the author of the selection, the title, the publisher, and the date of publication. The entries are listed in alphabetical order.

Here are two sample bibliographic entries. Check with your teacher or a librarian to learn how to credit other resources correctly.

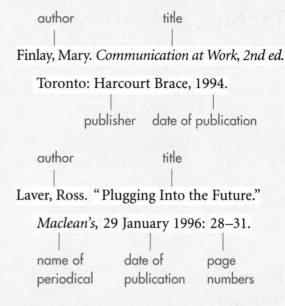

When your essay is complete, use the following checklist to decide whether or not it needs further revision. You may wish to ask a classmate to read over your essay and answer the same questions.

CHECKLIST: WRITING AN ESSAY

✔ Did my opening paragraph catch my reader's attention?

✔ Did each paragraph in the body of my essay present one main idea to support my thesis?

✔ Did I write at least one complete sentence to develop each supporting detail in the body of my essay?

✔ Did I show clearly how all of my ideas relate to one another and to my thesis?

✔ Did I present my ideas in the best order?

✔ Did I write a strong concluding paragraph?

✔ Have I corrected any errors of spelling, grammar, or punctuation?

✔ Have I included footnotes or end notes where needed? Have I included a bibliography?

Technical Writing

What Is Technical Writing?

The term **technical writing** describes much of the writing people do at work. Business letters, memos, science or technical reports, proposals, speeches, and manuals are all forms of technical writing. Technical writing communicates complex or precise information, such as definitions, descriptions, and instructions. For example, software designers write user manuals to tell people how to use their programs.

The Elements of Technical Writing

The following features are important in every kind of technical writing.

1. Clarity Technical writing should be clear and easy to understand. Here are some tips to help you keep your writing clear.

- Define any terms that you think the reader might not understand.
- Choose your words carefully to convey the specific meaning you intend.
- Organize your ideas in a logical order. (See page 141.)

2. Headings, Lists, and Visuals Headings, lists, and visuals can make your writing easier to understand.

A **heading** functions as a title for a section of text; it is placed on its own line at the beginning of the section. A reader can skim headings to find the relevant material.

Use a **list** to present a series of related items. Each item stands out, and the whole list is easy to find. Use a numbered list when the order of items is important; use bullets when the order doesn't matter.

List With Numbers	List With Bullets
To send a fax, follow these steps. 1. Place the document face down in the feeder. 2. Enter the fax number on the dial pad. 3. Press start.	The characteristics of an adult insect are • three pairs of legs • two pairs of wings • a body with three segments (head, thorax, abdomen)

Use a **visual** (also called a graphic) when it's too difficult to describe something in words. A visual might be a graph, a chart, a table, a photograph, a cartoon, or an illustration. It presents information mainly in the form of a picture or an image, although text is often added, such as labels or a title.

3. Audience Awareness Technical writing is usually addressed to a specific audience—to tell a customer how to assemble a product, to tell employees about changes in work schedules, or to apply for a job. As a technical writer, you must adapt your writing to meet the needs of your audience. Below are some important audience needs to consider.

Always read your writing from your audience's point of view. Think about the kinds of questions your audience might ask, and make sure you have answered them.

On the following pages is an excerpt from a grade 9 science report. Read it and assess the report using these questions.
- Are there any places where the report could be more clearly written?
- How well have the writers used headings, lists, and visuals?
- Have the writers demonstrated an awareness of their audience's needs and interests?
- Could you do this experiment by following their description of the procedure?
- Are there any steps where you might need more information?

The notes in the margins may give you some ideas.

Audience Need: Personal Interests	Audience Need: Required Information	Audience Need: Prior Knowledge
Appeal to your audience's interests, so that your writing is more likely to hold their attention.	Make sure you include all the information your audience needs to understand your message.	Make connections with what your audience already knows to help them understand new information.
Weak: I have made the following changes to the work schedule....	**Weak**: I was a student secretary at my high school.	**Weak**: In version six of WordPro, you use the numbered function keys for text formatting.
Better: So that every employee gets two days off over the July 1st weekend, I have made the following changes to the work schedule....	**Better**: As a student secretary at my high school, I answered phones, took messages, helped with filing, and ran errands for the school secretaries and teachers.	**Better**: In version six of WordPro, you may use the same text formatting commands as in version five, or you may use the numbered function keys across the top of your keyboard.

SCIENCE FAIR PROJECT: MALLEABILITY

–from an experiment written by Sean Keith and Sean Rosebrugh, students at Martingrove Collegiate.

PURPOSE

1 What is malleability?

To determine the range of malleability of five chosen metals. ①

Hypothesis

2 Sounds reasonable.

The treated metals such as the Galvanized Hot Dip and the High-Strength Plated Steel should be the least malleable as they are treated to be strong and not malleable. The less processed metals like the Bare Metal and the Brass should be the most malleable because they are not treated to be as stiff. ②

PROCEDURE ③

3 Headings are clear.

Materials Used

- 1 large metal vice
- 1 tea kettle
- 1 L water
- 6 stainless steel 2.5 inch by 1.25 inch bolts*
- 6 bare metal 2.5 inch by 1.25 inch bolts*
- 6 brass 2.5 inch by 1.25 inch bolts*
- 6 high-strength plated steel 2.5 inch by 1.25 inch bolts*
- 6 galvanized hot-dipped 2.5 inch by 1.25 inch bolts*
- 1 clothes peg
- 30 cm string
- 1 glue gun
- 1 egg timer

4 Is the shield just a piece of wood?

- 1 plywood shield 43 x 46.5 cm ④
- 1 pair safety goggles
- 1 pair protective gloves

[* These bolts are available only in Imperial sizes. There are no metric equivalents.]

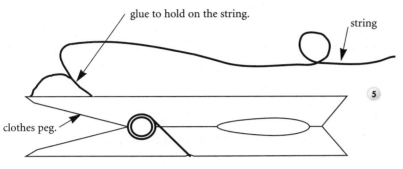

glue to hold on the string.

string

clothes peg.

5

Diagram 1.1
Apparatus for transportation of the bolts; used to stabilize the bolt in the vice safely

Steps in Room Temperature Trials
1. Safety goggles were put on.
2. A clothes peg was taken and placed around one of the bolts as shown in diagram 1.1.
3. The clothes peg was used to hold the bolt in place, 6 perpendicular to the walls of the vice.
4. The vice was tightened enough to secure the bolt without really pressing it.
5. Protective gloves were put on to prevent injury from projectile bolts and any other dangerous accidents.
6. The plywood shield was also prepared to protect against 7 the bolts ejected from the vice.
7. The bolt was tightened one quarter turn at a time while the number of quarter turns was noted.
8. The vice was continually turned until the bolt was unbendable or had snapped.
9. After the bolt was either broken or unyielding, it was removed from the vice and tagged appropriately by its material, number, and the temperature at which the test was performed.
10. The results were then recorded and converted into whole turns by dividing our number of quarter turns by four, 8 thus establishing a number of whole turns per bolt.
11. Steps one to ten were then repeated using three bolts of each bolt type.
12. The average from each bolt type was taken and that information was added to the record sheet.

5 I don't see the bolt in the diagram.

6 What does this look like?

7 Prepared how?

8 I wonder why they did this? Seems like a lot of work.

Steps in Heated Trials

1. Water was boiled in the kettle.
2. Safety equipment was re-applied. (9)

9 Same as page 165, I guess.

3. The vice was prepared to the appropriate size (to match the length of the bolt).
4. The string was then glue-gunned to the clothes peg so it could be lowered into the boiling water without burning people's hands. (10)

10 Good idea.

5. One of the bolts was put into the clothes peg's jaws.
6. The egg timer was set to run for thirty seconds, which was the duration of time that the bolt would be submersed. (11)

11 Submersed? I'll need to look it up.

7. The clothes peg was then lowered into the boiling water.
8. The timer was started simultaneously to the submersion of the bolt.
9. After the thirty seconds passed the timer sounded and the bolt was quickly removed from the kettle and placed into the vice.
10. Immediately after the bolt entered the vice, compression (12) began.

12 Sounds very efficient.

11. Again, the vice was tightened until the bolt was broken or incompressible. (13)

13 Isn't there an easier way to say this?

12. The bolt was removed from the vice by the clothes peg, tagged, and the results recorded.
13. Steps one through ten from the heated trial portion of the procedure were repeated using three bolts of each bolt type.
14. The results from each bolt type were averaged and that information was added to the record sheet. (14)

14 I think I could do the experiment.

Describing a Procedure

You will describe a simple process for the procedure section of a report.

Understanding the Task

A science report describes the procedure and results of an experiment. The exact form may vary, but all science reports have similar characteristics, and they share these characteristics with other types of reports. Science reports are

- divided into sections, each of which has a specific function
- organized logically to show the sequence of actions or events
- carefully written so that other people can understand and repeat the experiment

The following chart explains the function of each part of a science report.

Part	Function
Title	Describes the exact nature of the research.
Purpose	Explains the particular question the researcher wants to answer.
Procedure	Carefully describes each step of the experiment and all of the materials used.
Results	Presents the data generated by the research.
Conclusion	Analyzes and offers an explanation of the data.

Getting Ready

When you write a report, your writing should be clear so that your readers are left with no unanswered questions. Here are two skills you will need to use.

1. Defining You should provide a definition whenever you use a special word or phrase that your reader must understand in order to follow the rest of the report. For example, you should define the names of special equipment and any terminology that might be unfamiliar.

- A good definition gives another word that tells what kind of thing is being defined and then tells how the thing is unique.

  term   kind of thing

  A **pingo** is a hill found in the Arctic, consisting of a layer of soil with a mound of ice underneath.

  unique features

- You can also define something by comparing it to something the reader will probably recognize.

term
|
A wallaby is a marsupial that is much
like a kangaroo, but smaller.
                    |
                comparison

- Giving examples is another good way of
  defining a term.

  We conducted the experiment to

  see how common gases —————— term

  such as nitrogen, helium, ———— examples

  and carbon dioxide would react.
       |
    example

2. Describing The ability to write clear
descriptions is essential for many kinds of
technical writing. A detailed description of
the steps of an experiment is required in the
procedure section of a science report. Below
are some tips for writing good descriptions.

- Keep your audience in mind. Your
  descriptions should suit the knowledge
  your readers already have. Save the most
  detailed descriptions for objects and
  processes that may be new to your
  readers.

- Give precise measurements when necessary. If you must give more than one set
  of measurements, present them in a logical order, using a pattern such as top to
  bottom, left to right, or one object at a
  time.

- Start with a general statement, and then
  give specific details.

                general statement
                       |
A galvanometer is an instrument that

measures small electric currents. It

consists of two metal-tipped leads or

clips that can be attached |

to a source through which   specific
                               details
electricity flows. Between

the leads is a meter with a needle that |

indicates the strength and direction

of the electric current.

- If you are describing a process or procedure, divide it into steps and describe
  each step in the order in which it
  occurs. Use the past tense.

general statement
       |
We used litmus paper to test whether

the solution was an acid or a base.

First we stirred the solution to make

sure it was well mixed.— step 1

Next Suwanda held the litmus paper

by one end and dipped the other end

into the solution.— step 2

We observed the litmus paper change

colour — step 3   and recorded the

data in our chart. — step 4

- Sometimes it's better to use a visual instead of a lengthy or complicated verbal description.

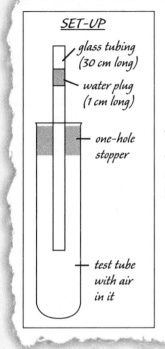

SET-UP

glass tubing
(30 cm long)

water plug
(1 cm long)

one-hole
stopper

test tube
with air
in it

We set up our equipment as shown in illustration #1.

Writing Your Description

Choose a simple procedure and describe it so that a younger brother or sister could repeat it. You might describe
- how to program a VCR
- how to prepare scrambled eggs and toast
- how to perform a simple experiment

Keep your readers in mind at all times, and define any terms they may not be familiar with. Describe each step of the process clearly, in simple language. Include any necessary safety precautions, especially for younger children.

When you have written your description, reread it to make sure that it is clear and the steps are easy to follow. Use the checklist below to assess your writing. You may want to ask a classmate, or a younger brother or sister, to read your procedure and answer the same questions.

CHECKLIST: DESCRIBING A PROCEDURE

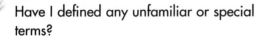

✔ Have I defined any unfamiliar or special terms?

✔ Have I included all of the steps in the procedure?

✔ Are the instructions clear and easy to follow?

✔ Have I left out any important information?

✔ Have I made connections to things my audience already knows?

✔ Could I use a visual to explain part of the process more clearly?

Writing a Résumé

LEARNING EXPECTATION
You will write a résumé.

Understanding the Task

When you apply for a job, you may have a short conversation with a store manager, or fill out a standard application form, or prepare a résumé to send in reply to an advertisement. If you use a résumé, it must speak for you. It must provide the employer with accurate information about your experience and your skills. This is your chance to say "This is who I am and what I can do for you."

There are many formats for résumés and letters of application, but they should always

- give employers the information they need, clearly and concisely.
- highlight the skills and experience that make you right for the job.
- be absolutely free of grammar and spelling errors! You want to impress the employer.

Getting Ready

These features of a résumé are designed to highlight the skills you have developed during school and extra-curricular activities.

1. Identification This appears at the top of the résumé and should include your name, address, and phone number. Include a fax number or e-mail address, if you have either. Make sure your name stands out!

TECHNOLOGY TIP

You can make your résumé stand out by giving it a unique design treatment using some of the different typefaces available in your word processing or desktop publishing software. You could use a special typeface for your name and address, for example, but make sure the typeface is easy to read.

2. Work and Volunteer Experience Identify two or three skills that will make you a good employee. Describe how you acquired each skill, and give evidence that you have used it.

3. Education Identify the name of your school, what year you are in, and any awards you have won. You can also list the courses in which you do best, and any courses you have taken, such as word processing or accounting, that relate directly to a job you might apply for.

Sample Résumé

Anton Rapp
1105 Butternut Ave., Burnaby, BC V4K 2Z9
(604) 555-1234

Work and Volunteer Experience

Organized and Responsible Leader
As an experienced outdoors person, I am trained to react quickly and efficiently while keeping people calm in a crisis. I received valuable YMCA leadership training and experience while on an extended canoeing expedition last summer. I have also had experience leading my own backpacking trips with friends.

Multi-Task Worker
I have experience baby-sitting, doing bicycle repairs, and helping people in my community. I have developed skills in dealing with the public, taking health and safety precautions, and organizing my time.

Computer Friendly
I have had considerable experience using Apple computers and PCs, and the Internet. My experience has shown that I learn new computer concepts quickly.

Education

I am in grade 10 at Westview Secondary School, receiving excellent grades in Physical Education (team and individual activities) and in English (verbal and written communication). So far this year I have maintained a 75% average.

Other Activities

- St. John Ambulance baby-sitting course, 1995
- 150 km YMCA canoeing expedition last summer as leader-in-training
- advanced skills in canoeing, hiking, and camping
- expect to qualify for Bronze Medallion (swimming) and Senior Resuscitation First Aid Certificate before summer
- My work experience includes baby-sitting, repairing bicycles, and doing yard work.

References

Dave Quann, Westview teacher (604) 555-1321 (school), (604) 555-5014 (home)
Meghan Jossa, neighbour (604) 555-7213 (office), (604) 555-3370 (home)

Skills		Personal Qualities	
repairing	selling	self-motivated	punctual
teaching	decision-making	accurate	organized
communicating	leading	responsible	outgoing
listening	performing	cooperative	helpful
cooperating	planning	dependable	tactful
supervising	scheduling	energetic	thorough
helping	problem-solving	hard-working	flexible
learning	speaking	enthusiastic	patient
organizing	building	imaginative	adaptable
writing	managing	positive	self-disciplined

Adapted from Mary Finlay, *Communication at Work, 2nd edition*, (Toronto: Harcourt Brace Canada, 1994), p. 137.

4. Other Activities List the clubs you belong to, any hobbies you have, and any other job-related skills you have learned.

5. References The best references are past employers who liked your work. Other good references are volunteer coordinators and teachers. Never use family members as references. Always ask permission before you use someone as a reference. If you prefer, you may say "References are available upon request" on your résumé, and bring a list of references to the interview.

TECHNOLOGY TIP

Using a word processing program, you can create a unique résumé for each job you seek. Prepare a file of descriptions for the Work and Volunteer Experience and Other Activities sections. Emphasize different skills and personal qualities. Then select the ones that best suit each job you apply for. Update the file with recently acquired skills.

Preparing Your Résumé

There are many reference books available on how to prepare for and write a winning résumé. Ask your librarian for help.

To prepare your own résumé

- List all of the important events in your life related to your education, work experience, and volunteer experience.
- List your hobbies, the clubs you've belonged to, and favourite activities.
- Brainstorm with a friend or family member to make sure you don't miss anything important.
- Describe each item on your list. Look at the Skills and Personal Qualities charts above and choose some words that best describe you. Include these words in your descriptions.
- Don't worry about using complete sentences; just jot down words and phrases that describe what you have learned and what you have done. Emphasize things you do well.

- Read your notes and highlight details that you think best demonstrate your skills and personal qualities. Circle any descriptions that seem really important or particularly well phrased. Then summarize these details in complete sentences.

Use the information in your summary to prepare a résumé following the model on page 171. Limit your résumé to one page, without making it look crowded. Proofread it to make sure that there are no errors in spelling or grammar. Finally, use the checklist below to assess your writing. Have a teacher, or another adult who knows you well, read your résumé and comment on it.

CHECKLIST: WRITING A RÉSUMÉ

✓ Did I include the most important skills I have learned?

✓ Did I include the most important information about my education, work experience, and volunteer experience?

✓ Did I correct any vague information in my résumé by adding brief descriptions or definitions?

✓ Did I give an accurate impression of who I am and what I can do?

✓ Did I include only positive information about myself?

✓ Did I eliminate all spelling and grammar errors?

✓ Did I make my résumé easy to read? Did the information stand out clearly on the page?

Writing a Letter of Application

You will write a letter of application for an advertised job.

Understanding the Task

There are two common types of letters of application.
- a response to an advertised job opening.
- a letter addressed to an employer you would like to work for, when no job has been advertised. This is often called a "cold call" letter.

Any letter sent to apply for a job must be neat and polite—and absolutely free of errors! It should tell the employer who you are and what you can do. The information should be written to appeal to the specific needs and interests of the employer. You may be an excellent trombone player, but this will interest employers only if they are looking for a musician or if you can show them that your musical training has helped you develop qualities that would be useful in their business.

Getting Ready

The purpose of a letter of application is to sell you and your abilities to an employer who does not know you. When responding to an ad, use the requirements mentioned in the ad to help you choose the information to highlight in your letter. Here are some of the features of a successful letter of application.

1. **Return Address** This gives your full name, address, and telephone number, as well as a fax number or an e-mail address, if you have either. Make sure the employer can contact you easily.

2. **Address and Salutation** Include the full company name and address of the employer, as well as the name and title of the contact person mentioned in the ad. If no name is mentioned, you could either phone and ask for a name, or address the letter to "Dear Sir or Madam."

3. **The Body of the Letter** Here you identify the job you are applying for and how you found out about it. Describe your skills and work experience, showing how they fit the needs of the job or the company. Don't repeat all the information from your résumé; just give a few important highlights. Include a short paragraph about your personal qualities and how they suit the needs of the job. Use formal language and be polite and concise, but also be positive and enthusiastic. Don't forget that your sentence structure and spelling should be perfect.

4. Action Here you ask for an interview. Or, if you're sending a "cold call" letter, offer to call the contact person at a specific time.

5. Final Salutation Be polite and always include both your signature and your full name in type.

TECHNOLOGY TIP

File your letter of application on computer. You can reuse the basic information when applying for other jobs.

Preparing Your Letter

Prepare a letter of application in response to the ad included here, or in response to an ad from your community. Make sure you highlight how your skills, experience, and personal qualities make you right for the job. When you've completed a first draft of your letter, assess it by using the following checklist. Also, have an adult such as a parent or your teacher read the letter and make comments on it.

This is the advertisement that student Anton Rapp answered in his letter of application on page 176.

Kidzville Amusement Park
Summer Jobs!!!

Are you a hard-working, enthusiastic individual looking for lots of Sun, Fun, and New Friendships? Then we'd like you to work at Kidzville Amusement Park. Great positions available in Food Service, Retail Sales, Rides, Game Operations, Grounds Crew, and Ticket Sales.

So if you're looking for more than an ordinary job...You're on!!!

Interviews begin in February...
Apply Now—See your guidance counsellor or give me a call at (604) 555-2345
Kelina Mueller, Human Resources Manager
Westly Amusements
90 Forward Ave.
Vancouver, BC V5X 2T7

Anton Rapp ①
1105 Butternut Ave., Burnaby, BC V4K 2Z9
Tel. (604) 555-1234   Fax (604) 555-9876

January 14, 1998

Ms. Kelina Mueller ②
Human Resources Manager
Westly Amusements
90 Forward Ave.
Vancouver, BC V5X 2T7

Dear Ms. Mueller:

I would like to apply for a summer job at Kidzville Amusement Park, as advertised at Westview Secondary School.

For the past two summers I have taken part in hiking, camping, and canoeing trips with the YMCA. ③ Last year I was a leader-in-training on a 150 km canoeing expedition. I have a proven ability to handle a crisis while keeping people calm and out of danger. I also have experience handling money, from setting and receiving payment for baby-sitting and yard work, to purchasing supplies for bicycle repairs and camping trips.

I am outgoing, responsible, and hard-working. I have a positive attitude and enjoy working with people and being outdoors.

I look forward to discussing with you in person how my skills and abilities would fit the various positions available at Kidzville Amusement Park. ④

Sincerely, ⑤

Anton Rapp

Anton Rapp

CHECKLIST: WRITING A LETTER OF APPLICATION

✔ Did my letter appeal to the needs identified in the ad?

✔ Did I describe my skills and experience clearly?

✔ Did I need to add any more descriptions or explanations?

✔ Did I express myself politely and use formal language?

✔ Did I sound positive and enthusiastic?

✔ Did I eliminate all spelling and grammar errors?

Writing Power Tools

As a writer, there is nothing more satisfying than having your work appreciated by an audience. But a writer must work hard to win that appreciation. The strategies in Making Your Writing Stronger will help you make your writing interesting, while the strategies in Making Grammar and Spelling Corrections will help you produce an error-free product.

Making Your Writing Stronger

WRITING POWERFUL LEADS

The opening few sentences of a piece of writing are the most important. You must engage your readers' interest.

> "I see the debate about using animals in medical research in stark terms. If you had to choose between saving a very cute dog or my equally cute, blond, brown-eyed daughter, whose life would you choose?"
>
> —from "Do We Need to Use Animals in Research?" by Jane McCabe

Jane McCabe lets us know what her subject is, and she tells us which side of the "debate" she is on and why. She also poses a question to engage our interest and sympathy.

Here are some strategies you can use to give your **essays** and **reports** a strong start.
- Surprise your audience with a fascinating fact or quotation.
- Ask your audience a challenging question.
- Engage your readers' emotions with a story about your life.

> "I was getting fed up with saying goodbye. One month five kids disappeared from my shrinking class at Copelin High School."
>
> —from "The Visitor" by Christine Pinsent-Johnson

Christine Pinsent-Johnson begins her story by showing us how sad Willy feels about saying goodbye to his friends.

Here are some strategies you can use to give your **stories** a powerful beginning.
- Open with a dialogue between two characters that introduces the conflict.
- Begin with a description of the setting that creates a mood.
- Start in the middle of a dramatic action scene.
- Introduce the main problem in the story through the thoughts of a narrator.

YOUR TURN

With a partner, read aloud the opening paragraphs of some of your pieces of writing. Discuss how you might make these openings more powerful. Then rewrite one of your opening paragraphs. Read your version aloud to a partner to get feedback.

MAKING YOUR CHARACTERS COME ALIVE

Characters are the centre of any story. If you can create living, breathing characters, your audience will want to read about them.

How you can bring your characters to life	Here's how Christine Pinsent-Johnson did it in "The Visitor"
Let your readers see the way your characters look, move, and dress.	"He just stood there, waiting, gripping on to that piece of paper as if it gave him the strength to stand."
Let your readers hear the thoughts and feelings of your characters.	"I hated it when he used my full name. It sounded so fake. As if he was trying too hard."
Let your readers hear your characters speak.	"'He must be some stunned to come wandering into a town full of hunters,' said Mr. Smith.... 'Don't he realize people here live all winter on a freezer full of his distant relatives?'"
Let your readers see the habits and personality traits of your characters.	"'Do you think it's a good idea to go out just before supper?' Dad asked, clearing his throat nervously." "He quietly cleared his throat. His first words didn't quite make it out."
Let your readers feel your characters' problems.	"I was getting fed up with saying goodbye.... I was witnessing the slow death of a town and there was nothing I or anyone else could do about it."

YOUR TURN

Write about a humorous or angry confrontation between two characters. Use at least two of the techniques described above to make your characters come to life.

USING COLOURFUL LANGUAGE

Try to use interesting nouns, verbs, and modifiers so your readers will not become confused or bored.

1. **Nouns** Using specific rather than general nouns makes your message clear. See how the following sentence is improved by changing one noun.

general noun

• I gasped when I turned the corner and saw the snake in the middle of the room.

specific noun

• I gasped when I turned the corner and saw the python in the middle of the room.

2. **Verbs** If you want to add some zip to your writing, look at the verbs you're using. Here are two sentences featuring the verb *walk*. See what happens to the sentences when the verb is changed.

Originals	Revisions
• Catriona pushed the rock aside and *walked* into the tomb.	• Catriona pushed the rock aside and *crept* into the tomb.
• Kim Thanh *walked* to the stage to accept the trophy.	• Kim Thanh *leapt up* to the stage to accept the trophy.

The new verbs create a mood in the sentences and give the reader a clearer picture of what is happening.

3. **Modifiers** Adjectives and adverbs are modifiers. They describe nouns and verbs, and some of the other parts of speech. You can use adjectives and adverbs to make your writing more interesting. Modifiers also help to create a mood in your writing. See how these sentences come to life with interesting modifiers.

Originals	Revisions
• Emily skied down the mountain. (no modifiers)	• Emily skied *aggressively* down the *treacherous* mountain. (modifiers add detail and excitement)
• I stretched out on the grass and gazed into the sky. (no modifiers)	• I stretched out on the *cool* grass and gazed into the *cloudless* sky. (modifiers create a pleasant mood)

YOUR TURN

In a sample of a partner's writing, choose one paragraph and circle the nouns and verbs. Are there nouns and verbs you could replace with more specific words? Could you add or change adjectives or adverbs to give your partner's writing more life? Explain your changes to your partner.

WRITING EFFECTIVE DIALOGUE

Read the dialogue that follows and think about what makes it work.

" 'My dears, you're not going to believe what I saw last night,' she [Mrs. Tilley] said breathlessly. 'I was out for my walk and when I rounded the corner of Ore Street I stared straight into the glaring red eyes of the devil itself.' "
—from "The Visitor" by Christine Pinsent-Johnson

The author breathes life into the character of Mrs. Tilley with this speech. She reveals herself as excitable, talkative, and superstitious. The author also uses this speech to add humour to the story and to introduce some important information about the visitor.

Here are some things to remember when you write dialogue.

- Your dialogue should sound like real people speaking. You can use slang, incomplete sentences, dialect, and imperfect grammar. To check if your dialogue sounds like real speech, read it out loud.
- Your dialogue should always serve a clear purpose: to show conflict or action, to reveal character traits, or to provide information.
- Keep your speeches fairly short. The dialogue should move back and forth among the characters.
- Use dialogue to emphasize important scenes or turning points in your story.

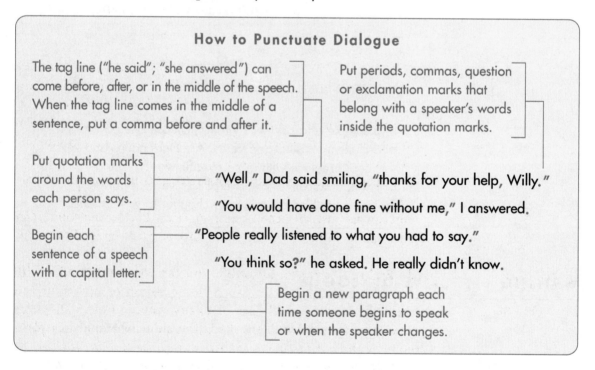

How to Punctuate Dialogue

The tag line ("he said"; "she answered") can come before, after, or in the middle of the speech. When the tag line comes in the middle of a sentence, put a comma before and after it.

Put periods, commas, question or exclamation marks that belong with a speaker's words inside the quotation marks.

Put quotation marks around the words each person says.

Begin each sentence of a speech with a capital letter.

"Well," Dad said smiling, "thanks for your help, Willy."

"You would have done fine without me," I answered.

"People really listened to what you had to say."

"You think so?" he asked. He really didn't know.

Begin a new paragraph each time someone begins to speak or when the speaker changes.

YOUR TURN

Choose a story you have written and look for a part that you could improve by adding dialogue. Rewrite the scene with your characters having a conversation. Make sure the dialogue adds interest to your story.

WRITING EFFECTIVE ENDINGS

Have you ever been disappointed by the ending of a book, an essay, a story, or a movie? Good writing, in both fiction and non-fiction, leaves a reader with a sense of satisfaction and completion. You may need to try several different endings to a piece of writing before you find one that feels right. Here are three kinds of endings to try.

1. **Complete the circle.** In "The Visitor," the author opens the story with Willy worrying about students leaving his class as families move away from Copelin. The story ends with this sentence: "Copelin would never be the same as it once was, but at least it wouldn't become a forgotten ghost town, and maybe I wouldn't be the only one left by the time I graduated from high school." The story begins and ends with the narrator's thoughts about school.

You can also use this technique in an essay. The ending could refer back to the opinion, quotation, or anecdote that opened the essay.

2. **End at a jumping-off point.** You can leave your reader with something to think about, such as a question or an action you think the reader should take. In a story, you can leave a character facing a choice or challenge. But if you do this, you must plant enough clues throughout the story to make the answer easy to predict, or your reader will not be satisfied.

3. **Summarize your observations.** You can restate the main points you have made in your essay, or just the most important one. You

can also sum up a lesson you learned for the ending to a personal narrative, or the lesson a character learned for the ending to a story.

YOUR TURN

With a partner, analyze the endings of some short stories, essays, or magazine and newspaper articles. Note how the writers ended each selection. Then take a piece of your own writing and discuss different ways of ending it.

SENTENCE VARIETY AND SENTENCE COMBINING

When all of your sentences sound alike, your writing may be boring to read. Here are some suggestions for you to keep in mind when revising your sentences.

Don't start every sentence the same way. It's easy to get stuck in a rut and write a string of sentences like these, with the same word at the beginning of every sentence.

> I interviewed a firefighter to find out about her job. I learned about the many dangers a firefighter faces. I thought the worst dangers would be fire and heat. I was surprised to find out that smoke and toxic gases are just as threatening.

Here are two ways to change sentences like these.

1. Delete the repeated word.

Original	Revision
• I learned about the many dangers a firefighter faces.	• A firefighter faces many dangers.

2. Move the repeated word.

Original	Revision
• I thought the worst dangers would be fire and heat.	• The worst dangers would be fire and heat, I thought.

One way to add variety to your writing is to combine two or more sentences to create new sentences. Here are a few sentence-combining techniques.

Technique #1: Look for words in related sentences that are the same or similar. Create a new sentence so you don't have to repeat these words.

same subject

• The beaver listened attentively. The beaver did not move or make a sound.

Combined: The beaver listened attentively without moving or making a sound.

verbs are the same or similar

• Evan ate a sandwich. He munched an apple. He ate two cookies.

Combined: Evan munched a sandwich, an apple, and two cookies.

Technique #2: Join short, related sentences to create longer sentences. When you join sentences, you must add words to show how the two sentences relate to each other. These words are called **conjunctions**.

- Clouds covered the sky. A cold wind swept down from the north.

Combined: Clouds covered the sky, and a cold wind swept down from the north.

- Courtney shouted as loudly as she could. No one seemed to hear.

Combined: Courtney shouted as loudly as she could, but no one seemed to hear.

- Maggie slept soundly. The morning sun shone through her window.

Combined: Maggie slept soundly, even though the morning sun shone through her window.

- Leon sat out of the volleyball game. He had a sprained ankle.

Combined: Because Leon had a sprained ankle, he sat out of the volleyball game.

 Notice that you can change the order of the sentences when you combine them. See page 217 for more about conjunctions.

Technique #3: Identify the important words in related sentences and cut out the ones that don't say very much. Use the important words to create a new sentence. This technique will also help you to be more concise.

- Stan sat down heavily on the chair. The chair was shaky. It collapsed under Stan's weight.   important ideas

Combined: Stan sat down heavily on the shaky chair, and it collapsed.

Technique #4: Identify the main sentence and use phrases to express some of the ideas in related sentences. Add the phrases to the main sentence.

main sentence

• The tall ship sailed into the harbour. Its flags were flying. The captain was at the wheel.

phrase

Combined: Its flags flying, the tall ship sailed into the harbour with the captain at the wheel.

phrase

For more information about phrases in sentences, see page 195.

YOUR TURN

With a partner, select a paragraph of your own writing that has at least five sentences. Look at how you began each sentence. If one word appears two or three times in a row, revise your sentences to avoid the repetition. Then decide whether you can combine any two or more sentences into one. Compare your original and revised paragraphs. Decide whether your changes are an improvement.

WHEN TO START A NEW PARAGRAPH

Readers expect a long piece of writing to be divided into paragraphs. The beginning of a new paragraph tells the reader to expect a change of some kind. Here are some of the changes you should signal by starting new a paragraph.

1. A New Topic Use a new paragraph when you move from one topic to another. In the story "The Visitor," the author describes the condition of one of the streets in Copelin. When she starts to describe the homes on the street, she starts a new paragraph.

> Most of the snow had washed away except for some skeletal remains along the edges of the street and in the ditches. Everyone kept saying they were lucky it was such a mild winter because there was no money for snowplowing. But now the potholes needed to be filled, and there was no money for that either.
>
> Out of a dozen homes on the street five were empty. At the Purdys' house the front door was wide open...

2. A Change of Setting: Time or Place Use a new paragraph to warn your readers about a shift to a new time or place. This works best when the change is small—from morning to afternoon, or from inside to outside. If you want to warn your readers about a larger change, put extra space and a few asterisks (*) or other symbols between the paragraphs. You can see this technique in the short story "The Visitor" on page 17.

3. To Give Emphasis To emphasize an idea or action, you can put it in a very short paragraph all by itself. This is a powerful technique, but don't use it too often or it will lose its power. Cam Cole uses this technique in the first paragraph of "9.84," on page 73.

4. A New Speaker Start a new paragraph whenever someone begins to speak or when the speaker changes. For more about dialogue, see page 181.

YOUR TURN

Flip through a book and find a page with several short paragraphs. Rewrite some or all of the page as one solid paragraph, and then exchange it for a similar paragraph prepared by a classmate. Mark where you think each new paragraph should begin. Check your ideas against the original.

Editing means making changes to your writing to improve it. Editing and rewriting are important parts of the writing process. Professional writers will tell you that writing is actually one-tenth writing and nine-tenths rewriting.

Editing Your Own Work

The hardest part of editing your own work is trying to see it with fresh eyes. If possible, put it away for at least a day. When you read it again, pretend that it's someone else's work. Ask yourself "How can I make this better?" Look at the Revising stage of the writing process, on page 137.

Read your work several times and mark
- places where your meaning is not clear
- words, sentences, or paragraphs that seem out of order
- words, sentences, or paragraphs to delete
- places where more information or explanation is needed

Read your work several times, each time looking for something different. Here are some things to look for along with some editing techniques.

1. Read for the big picture. Read your whole piece and think about the meaning and purpose of what you've written. Ask
- Does it make sense?
- What do I like or dislike?
- Is my main idea clear? If not, how can I make it clearer?
- Have I said everything that I need to say?

2. Read aloud. Read your work aloud or tape-record it and play it back. Listen to how your writing sounds. Ask
- Do all of my sentences read smoothly?
- Do any of them sound awkward or incomplete?
- Did I use too many short, choppy sentences?
- Are any of my sentences too long and confusing?

3. Read it in pieces. Read each paragraph separately and use the paragraph checklist on page 146, to assess them. Then look at all of the paragraphs together to see if they are in the best possible order.

TECHNOLOGY TIP

If you prepare your work on a computer, you can complete your editing stages very quickly using the cut and paste functions.

4. Write a clean copy. After you have read your work several times, make the changes you think are necessary, and produce a clean copy of your revised work. Then read it again to see how your changes worked. If you have time, you may revise and rewrite your work several times.

Proofreading

To **proofread** your work, you read it over carefully to correct errors in punctuation, sentence structure, grammar, word choice, and spelling.

Read it slowly. Concentrate on each word in your writing. It may help to read it aloud again. Or you could point to each word on the page, hold a ruler under each line as you read, or read your work from the end to the beginning, one word at a time. Remember, people often see what they meant to write rather than what's actually written on the page. Be careful!

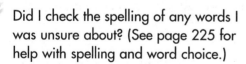

CHECKLIST: PROOFREADING

✔ Did I check the spelling of any words I was unsure about? (See page 225 for help with spelling and word choice.)

✔ Did I choose words that express my thoughts clearly?

✔ Did each of my sentences end with a punctuation mark?

✔ Are all of my sentences complete?

✔ Did I use a variety of sentence lengths?

✔ Did I use quotation marks for dialogue and quotations? (See page 219 for help with punctuation.)

✔ Did I either leave a blank line before each paragraph or indent each paragraph?

✔ Did I capitalize the first word in each sentence, and all proper nouns and titles?

Here is a sample of some student writing, with editing suggestions and proofreading marks on it.

Work, by Danielle Norquay

What would our world be like if ~~it didn't consist of~~ money ~~it would feel~~
it weren't run by *Life would be very different from what it is now.* ?

~~pretty weird.~~ But ~~this is not the case,~~ our world ~~does consist of~~ money. ~~Mostly~~
(What is "this"? Reword? Delete?) *is run by* *(is "consist" the right word?)* *Almost*

every thing that we do has a price.

~~Hello,~~ now how do we get money? ~~(Well if you think a little you will discover that~~
(Wrong tone.) *(Too many words that don't say very much)*

~~you need~~ to work to get money, and that is what I am going to ~~talk~~ about, work.
We all know we have *write*

> **YOUR TURN**
>
> Choose a short piece of your own writing. Follow the editing steps described on pages 189–190. Then show your first draft and revised drafts to a classmate to see how much your editing improved your original work.

EDITING WITH YOUR PEERS

One of the best ways to edit your writing is to have someone else read your work, someone who can look at it from a different point of view. You only really know your writing is good if someone else reads and understands it. Every writer needs an editor! Below are some peer editing techniques and tips.

1. **Reading Aloud** A good way to begin a peer editing session is to read the work aloud. If you are reading your own work, read slowly and clearly. If you are listening to someone else's work,

listen carefully and take notes during or after the reading. Concentrate on the overall effect of the work. Does it make sense? Do the ideas follow each other naturally?

2. Editing One-on-One Give your work to one other person to read and comment on. If you are reading someone's work, you can
- discuss the work informally with the writer
- jot notes directly on the page
- write longer comments on a separate piece of paper

3. Editing With a Group Give copies of your work to a group of classmates and have each respond as in Editing One-on-One.

When editing with a partner or a group, you must be polite and open-minded. Use the PQP approach (see next page).

Tips for the Writer

- Don't make excuses for your work or blame the editor for not understanding.
- Tell your editors the kind of help you want. Do you want them to look at the big picture or the details? To assess your arguments or your organization? Be specific.
- Tell your editors about any concerns or questions you have about your writing.
- Listen carefully to what your editors tell you about your work and make notes.
- Don't interrupt your editors or argue with them.
- Ask questions if you don't understand an editor's comments.
- Think carefully about all your editors' comments. Remember, they are making suggestions. You don't have to change anything you don't want to change.

Tips for the Editor

- Listen carefully as a writer reads a piece of writing.
- When you read the work yourself, follow the suggestions for editing your own work and proofreading.

- When you respond to a writer, either in discussion or in writing, use the Praise/Question/Polish (PQP) approach.

The PQP Approach

Praise
- Always begin by saying something positive about the work.
- Make sure that your comments are helpful to the writer rather than simply critical. Explain why you are making them.

Question
- Ask the writer questions about any part of the writing that isn't clear.
- Be polite. For instance, use phrases like "What do you mean when you say...?" "How do you think you could...?" "It seems to me that...." "Did you consider...?" and "Are you happy with...?"

Polish
- Give the kind of feedback the writer requested.
- Be as specific as possible. Point out exact places that you think need improving and give examples of what you mean. Explain why you think they need improving.

YOUR TURN

Choose an editing partner or form an editing group. Then choose a piece of writing you have had trouble with. Read your work to your partner or group, and follow the steps for editing with your peers.

Making Grammar and Spelling Corrections

HOW SENTENCES WORK

Grammar is a set of rules that explain how words are put together to form sentences. These rules were developed to help people talk about language and were never intended to be confusing. Grammar errors make your writing harder to understand. You don't need to memorize a lot of grammar rules. You do need to know how to fix a problem when you, your classmates, or your teacher finds one.

It's easy to describe what a sentence looks like—it begins with a **capital letter** and ends with a **period**, a **question mark**, or an **exclamation mark**. However, it's a little trickier to say what a sentence *is*. All three of the following examples look like sentences, but only one of them really is a sentence.

1. That grey mouse.
2. An owl hunts for food.
3. Washed the countryside with colour.

You probably know that the second example is a sentence, while the other two are not. But *how* do you know? Why is example 2 different from the others?

Subjects and Predicates

A sentence must have two parts: a **subject** and a **predicate**.

The **subject** usually comes first and tells the reader who or what the sentence is about. The **predicate** usually comes second and tells the reader what the subject is doing. A sentence uses a subject and predicate to express only one complete thought.

$$\text{a sentence} \quad = \quad \text{subject} \quad + \quad \text{predicate} \quad = \quad \text{a complete thought}$$

An owl   hunts for food.

Now you can explain why examples 1 and 3 above are not sentences. Example 1 does not have a predicate, and example 3 does not have a subject.

Below are some sentences that show variations of the subject-plus-predicate sentence structure.

Subject +	Predicate
Jandra	leaves school.
She	meets her friends Carmine and Scott.
Carmine, a figure skater,	is carrying a large sports bag.
Jandra and Scott	walk to the rink with Carmine to watch her practice.
Jandra	photographs Carmine's routine for the school yearbook.
Carmine	spins and jumps without falling.

The sentences in the chart above show that longer sentences still fit the subject-plus-predicate pattern.

Phrases and Clauses

Most of the sentences you read or write are more complicated than "Jandra leaves school." Writers use phrases and clauses to build longer, more detailed sentences.

A **phrase** is a group of words that work together. But a phrase is not a sentence, because it is missing a subject, a predicate, or both.

Below are a few sentences with phrases in them. Notice that a phrase can appear at the beginning, in the middle, or at the end of a sentence. Each phrase is highlighted, and the arrows show whether the phrase belongs with the subject or the predicate.

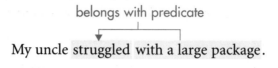

My uncle struggled with a large package.

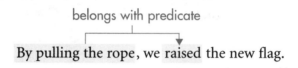

Shawna, our wilderness guide, lit the campfire.

belongs with predicate

By pulling the rope, we raised the new flag.

A **clause** is also a group of words that work together. But a clause does have both a subject and a predicate. There are two kinds of clauses. The first kind can stand on its own as a sentence. Because it doesn't need any help, it is called an **independent clause**.

The second kind of clause does not make sense unless it is joined with an independent clause. Because it needs help, it is called a **dependent clause**. Although a dependent clause has both a subject and a predicate, it does not express a complete thought so it is not a sentence.

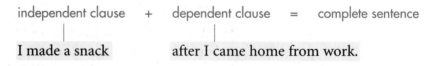

independent clause + dependent clause = complete sentence

I made a snack   after I came home from work.

Notice that the dependent clause "after I came home from work" does not make sense by itself.

A simple sentence is the same as an independent clause. More complicated sentences contain combinations of clauses and phrases. Here are some examples.

independent clause

I made lunch.

independent clause • phrase

Mike fixed the computer by replacing the power supply.

independent clause • phrase • independent clause

There was a party at Sharon's house, but I couldn't go.

dependent clause • independent clause

Because Taslim trained hard, she was the leading scorer on her team.

phrase

YOUR TURN

For each sentence below, identify the independent and dependent clauses. Remember that each clause will have its own subject and predicate.
1. Elton John and Paul Simon are my parents' favourite musicians.
2. My parents like to listen to the radio, but I would rather listen to my CDs.
3. I have to use my parents' CD player because I don't have one of my own.
4. They don't like my music, so I don't get to play my CDs very often.
5. If I can get a job, maybe I'll be able to buy my own CD player.

To identify more phrases and clauses, try analyzing some of your own writing. Discuss your conclusions with a partner.

If you are struggling with a grammar problem, you've come to the right place for help. This section explains 10 of the most common grammar errors and how to fix them.

Error 1: Run-On Sentences

In a run-on sentence, many ideas have been put together in one sentence, without correct punctuation.

What a Run-On Sentence Looks Like

> There was a blizzard overnight, the snowplows were out early by morning most of the roads were clear enough for safe driving.

Repairing the Problem
Your reader may have trouble keeping track of all the separate ideas in a run-on sentence. To repair the sentence, you must separate the ideas and add the correct punctuation.

Repair #1: Create three short sentences by using periods to separate each idea or independent clause.

> There was a blizzard overnight. The snowplows were out early. By morning, most of the roads were clear enough for safe driving.

Repair #2: Use a conjunction (words like *and, or, but, because, so, since*) to join some of the ideas, and a separate sentence to highlight the most important idea. In these two samples, the writer chose different ideas to highlight.

> There was a blizzard overnight. The snowplows were out early, and by morning most of the roads were clear enough for safe driving.

Because there was a blizzard overnight, the snowplows were out early. By morning most of the roads were clear enough for safe driving.

Sentences for You to Repair

Revise these sentences to separate the ideas.

1. I finished my homework and went to the mall, Lana and Phillip were watching the fashion show then I came home.
2. We brought the sausage into the house Michael wanted to check out how much we got, the dog was jumping up and down.
3. At the end of camp I packed my bags we all got on the train, I couldn't find my wallet.

 For more information about conjunctions, see page 217. For more information about clauses, see page 196.

Error 2: Sentence Fragments

A sentence fragment is a group of words that is punctuated like a sentence, but isn't a complete sentence.

What Sentence Fragments Look Like

Ate the Slurpee. (no subject)

That wiggly puppy. (no predicate)

If I hadn't dropped the Slurpee. (no independent clause)

Repairing the Problem

A sentence fragment won't make sense to your reader, because some information is missing. To repair the sentence, you must add the missing information.

Repair #1: Add a subject to complete the idea in the sentence.

My new puppy ate the Slurpee.

Repair #2: Add a predicate to complete the idea in the sentence.

That wiggly puppy jumped right out of my hands.

Repair #3: Add an independent clause to complete the idea in the sentence.

> If I hadn't dropped the Slurpee, **my puppy wouldn't have eaten it.**

Sentences for You to Repair

Revise these sentences to add the missing parts.

1. That gorgeous new suede jacket.
2. If she could score the next goal.
3. Howled at the moon all night.

You can read more about subjects, predicates, and independent clauses on pages 194–197.

Error 3: Sentences With Too Many or Too Few Commas

A sentence with too many commas is choppy and awkward to read. A sentence with too few commas has all its information jumbled together.

What Too Many Commas Looks Like

> The camping trip, was a disaster, because of the lousy weather.

> "Well," he said, "I just don't, quite, understand," as he read the instructions.

What Too Few Commas Looks Like

> For the hike to Silver Peak we brought juice bottled water granola mix and cookies.

> The lousy weather caused by a distant hurricane ruined our family picnic.

> David likes to wear bright outrageous and unusual ties.

Repairing the Problem

Commas show your reader when to pause and which parts of the sentence work together. To repair a sentence that has a problem with commas, read it out loud. When you pause naturally as you read, you probably need a comma. If a pause seems unnatural, you probably don't need a comma.

Repair #1: Look for lists of words that work in a series. These words should be separated by commas.

> For the hike to Silver Peak we brought **juice, bottled water, granola mix, and cookies**.

> David likes to wear **bright, outrageous, and unusual** ties.

Repair #2: Look for phrases or dependent clauses that add information to the main idea in the sentence. These may sometimes be separated by commas.

> **For the hike to Silver Peak** we brought juice, bottled water, granola mix, and cookies.

> The lousy weather, **caused by a distant hurricane**, ruined our family picnic.

Repair #3: Look for the subject and the verb in a sentence. These should not be separated by one comma. You can separate them by a phrase or a clause, but the phrase or clause must have a comma before and after it.

PUNCTUATION TIP

*The comma after "disaster" was deleted because a pause there felt unnatural.

       subject   verb

The camping trip was a disaster* because of the lousy weather.

    subject   verb

BUT: **The camping trip**, which I never wanted to take, **was** a disaster because of the lousy weather.

Repair #4: If a sentence seems to have too many commas, but you're not sure which ones to delete, try rephrasing the sentence to avoid commas.

> He read the instructions and said, "Well, I just don't quite understand."

> The camping trip was a disaster. We had lousy weather the whole time.

Sentences for You to Repair

Revise these sentences so there are neither too many nor too few commas.

1. "Before you leave the rehearsal can I get your coat?" he whispered to his new friend.
2. After you buy the apples peel them cut them in quarters take out the core and put them in the pot.
3. My youngest sister, is coming to the concert.
4. The fourth man from the left who is standing on my hat should move.
5. Meagan, the president, of the debating club, called a meeting, to discuss the upcoming competition.

For more about commas, see page 220.

Error 4: Vague Pronoun References

Pronouns are used to replace nouns. But sometimes it's not clear which noun the pronoun replaces. This is called a vague pronoun reference.

What a Vague Pronoun Reference Looks Like

?

Ashley caught up with **Kimiko** in the hall and started talking about the party. **She** became very excited.

Repairing the Problem

With a vague pronoun reference, your reader may not be sure whom or what the pronoun identifies. To repair the sentence, you must make the pronoun reference clear.

Repair #1: Replace the pronoun with the correct noun. This simple solution always works.

> Ashley caught up with Kimiko in the hall and started talking about the party. **Ashley** became very excited.

Repair #2: Rephrase the sentence so that there is no confusion about which noun the pronoun replaces.

> Ashley became very excited as **she** caught up with Kimiko in the hall and started talking about the party.

Repair #3: Rewrite the sentence to get rid of the pronoun.

> Ashley became very excited while talking to Kimiko about the party.

Sentences for You to Repair

Revise these sentences so there is no confusion about which noun the pronoun replaces. For more about pronouns, see page 213.

1. Kyle told Nathan that he was late for practice.
2. Nan put the CD in the player and noticed it was damaged.
3. Wylita had to finish her homework, baby-sit her little brother, and start cooking dinner. She had never done this before.

Error 5: Wrong Pronoun—Number, Gender, or Person

If the wrong pronoun is used to replace a noun, it may be unclear whom or what the pronoun identifies.

What the Wrong Pronoun Looks Like

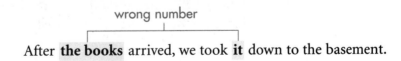

wrong number

After **the books** arrived, we took **it** down to the basement.

wrong gender

Margot says that **he** will drive today.

wrong person

Dustin and Marie thought the movie was terrific because **you** really got involved with the action.

Repairing the Problem

When you use the wrong pronoun, your reader may find a sentence confusing. For example, in the second sentence above, a reader might well ask, "Who is *he?*" To repair the sentence, you have to make sure that the pronoun you use agrees with the noun it replaces in these three ways.

Number refers to singular (*I*) and plural (*we*) pronouns.

Gender refers to masculine (*he*), feminine (*she*), and neuter (*it*) pronouns.

Person is like point of view in a story (see page 118). It refers to first-person (*I*), second-person (*you*), and third-person (*he/she*) pronouns.

Repair #1: Change the pronoun so it agrees with the noun it replaces.

plural   plural

After **the books** arrived, we took **them** down to the basement.

feminine   feminine

Margot says that **she** will drive today.

third person   third person

Dustin and Marie thought the movie was terrific because **they** really got involved with the action.

Repair #2: If the pronoun is really the one you want to use, then rephrase the sentence to clarify what you mean.

singular   singular

After **the box** of books arrived, we took **it** down to the basement.

Sentences for You to Repair

Revise these sentences so the pronoun agrees with the number, gender, and person of the noun it replaces.

1. Kim and Lila aren't living here anymore, because you don't get enough to eat.
2. These rings will belong to Edward when his dad doesn't wear it anymore.
3. When Sherry moved away, she forgot about her old friends and never called her anymore.
4. The moving van will be packed with the contents from three homes before them takes off.

Need more help? Read about pronouns on pages 213–214.

Error 6: Wrong Pronoun—Function

Sometimes writers choose the wrong kind of pronoun to serve a particular function in a sentence. It's a bit like hitting the brakes instead of the gas pedal.

What the Wrong Pronoun Looks Like

Us girls are going to the concert tonight.

My neighbour gave the tickets to Jeff and **I.**

Where's **me** hat?

Repairing the Problem

Sentences with errors in pronoun function will seem sloppy to your reader. To repair the sentence, you must identify the function the pronoun is supposed to serve in the sentence and then choose the correct one. These are three of the most common functions that pronouns serve.

1. Some pronouns are subjects: **I** am running. **She** went to school.
2. Some pronouns are objects: Sharlene gave the book to **him.** Guy asked **me** to dance.
3. Some pronouns show possession: This is **my** new CD. Everyone wants **their** autographs.

Repair #1: Identify the function the pronoun serves in the sentence and use the correct type of pronoun. These questions should help.
- Is the pronoun doing something? If so, it's probably a subject.
- Is something happening to the pronoun? If so, it's probably an object.
- Does the pronoun show who owns something? If so, it's possessive.

subject
|
We girls are going to the concert tonight.

object
|
My neighbour gave the tickets to Jeff and me.

possessive
|
Where's my hat?

Repair #2: If the pronoun is joined to another noun or pronoun by "and," try rephrasing the sentence using the pronoun by itself. You will probably know immediately which one sounds right.

My neighbour gave   OR   My neighbour gave
the tickets to I.   the tickets to me.

The second version sounds right, so the sentence should be:

My neighbour gave the tickets to Jeff and me.

Sentences for You to Repair
Revise these sentences so they have the correct pronoun.
1. Do you want to come with John and I to the movies?
2. The guests put them coats in the closet.
3. Her and my uncle are planning to open a new store next month.
4. The final goals were scored by he and Deb.

For more about pronouns and their functions, see pages 213–214.

Error 7: Subject/Verb Disagreement

If the subject and verb in a sentence don't agree, it may not be clear if the sentence is about one or more than one person or thing.

What This Type of Subject/Verb Disagreement Looks Like

    plural   singular

The children takes a nap in the afternoon.

    singular   plural

The protest march are coming right down our street.

Repairing the Problem

If the subject and verb in a sentence do not agree, the reader may be unsure which is correct, the subject or the verb. To repair the sentence, you must make the subject and verb agree with each other. If the subject is singular, the verb must be singular. If the subject is plural, the verb must be plural.

Repair #1: Change the verb so it agrees with the noun.

    plural   plural

The children take a nap in the afternoon.

    singular   singular

The protest march is coming right down our street.

Repair #2: Change the noun so it agrees with the verb.

    singular singular

The child takes a nap in the afternoon.

    plural   plural

The protest marchers are coming right down our street.

Sentences for You to Repair

Revise these sentences so the subjects agree with the verbs.

1. These leaves is the prettiest one of the bunch.
2. The new judo course have a lot of students from our class.
3. The dishes was broken when the table fell.

For more information about verbs, see page 214.

Error 8: Subject/Verb Disagreement— Compound Subjects

In a sentence where the subject is made up of two nouns or pronouns joined by *or, nor,* or *and,* it may not be clear whether the verb should be plural or singular.

What This Type of Subject/Verb Disagreement Looks Like

Jack and Jill **goes** to the store to buy some mineral water.

Either the actors or the director **were** responsible for the new dialogue.

Neither the barn nor the animals **was** hurt by the flood.

Repairing the Problem

If a compound subject does not agree with its verb, the reader may be unsure which is correct, the subject or the verb. To repair the sentence, you must make the compound subject agree with its verb.

Repair #1: When a compound subject is joined by **and**, you always use a plural verb.

plural

Jack **and** Jill **go** to the store to buy some mineral water.

Repair #2: When a compound subject is joined by **or** or **nor**, the verb must agree with the closest part of the subject.

singular

Neither the animals **nor** the **barn was** hurt by the flood.

plural

Neither the barn **nor** the **animals were** hurt by the flood.

Sentences for You to Repair

Revise these sentences so the compound subjects agree with the verbs.

1. Max, Elspeth, and I wants to sign up for gymnastics this fall.
2. Neither the department head nor the other teachers has a spare period today.
3. Either the singer or the piano player were off beat.
4. You and your family is coming to our place tomorrow evening.

For more about verbs, see page 214.

Error 9: Subject/Verb Disagreement— When Information Separates Them

When a group of words, such as a phrase or a dependent clause, separates the subject from the verb, it may not be clear whether the verb should be singular or plural.

What This Type of Subject/Verb Disagreement Looks Like

dependent clause

My friends, **who all belong to the same club, was** down at the snowboarding demonstration yesterday.

phrase

The box **for the in-line skates were** on the shelf.

Repairing the Problem

If the verb does not agree with the subject of the sentence, your reader may not be sure which is correct, the subject or the verb. To repair the sentence, you must identify the subject of the sentence and the main verb in the predicate, and make sure they agree.

Repair #1: Change the verb to agree with the subject of the sentence.

subject, plural   main verb, plural

My friends, who all belong to the same club, **were** down at the snowboarding demonstration yesterday.

subject, singular   singular

The box for the in-line skates **was** on the shelf.

Repair #2: To avoid confusion, rephrase the sentence so the subject is closer to the verb.

My **friends were** down at the snowboarding demonstration yesterday. We all belong to the same club.

The in-line **skates are** in a box on the shelf.

Sentences for You to Repair

Revise these sentences so the subjects and verbs agree.
1. The list of young men and women are posted in the principal's office.
2. The bowls that are full of spaghetti is at the end of the table.
3. The laneway that runs behind all those old houses were being dug up for repair.

Need more help with subject/verb agreement? See pages 207-209.

Error 10: Using the Wrong Modifier

Adjectives describe nouns and pronouns. Adverbs describe verbs, adjectives, and other adverbs. When you use an adjective instead of an adverb, the sentence sounds wrong and the meaning may be unclear.

What Wrong Modifiers Look Like

You did **good** on that test.

She ran **real** hard in that race.

He ate an **unusual** large meal.

Repairing the Problem

If you use an adjective where you should use an adverb, a reader may think you are a sloppy writer. To repair the sentence, you must replace the adjective with an adverb.

Repair #1: Find the modifiers in a sentence and identify which words they describe. If the word is a noun or a pronoun, make the modifier an adjective. Otherwise, use an adverb.

modifies a verb

You **did well** on that test.

modifies another adverb

She ran **really hard** in that race.

modifies an adjective

He ate an **unusually large** meal.

Repair #2: If you are unsure about how to correct the modifier, try rephrasing the sentence so it is easier to decide which modifier to use or so that you don't need a modifier.

You got an A on that test.

She ran a powerful race.

He ate a huge meal.

Sentences for You to Repair

Revise these sentences so they use the correct modifiers.
1. My dog behaved miserable at Dog Obedience School.
2. Twyla talked real softly at the speech contest.
3. That sweater goes perfect with Kelina's slacks.
4. The skate blade made a horrible deep cut in Jay's leg.

Need more help? See information about adjectives on page 215 and about adverbs on page 216.

This section gives you more information about the parts of speech and about punctuation.

Parts of Speech

Every word in a sentence has a function. In total, there are eight functions, which are known as the eight parts of speech. The sentence below shows these eight parts of speech.

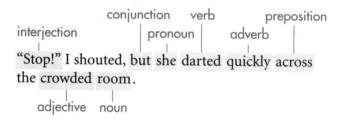

This section gives the definitions for the eight parts of speech and explains how they are used in sentences.

1. Nouns

A **noun** names a person, place, thing, idea, or quality.

Person	Place	Thing	Idea/Quality
Jean	Regina	boxes	colour
Chief Cusak	Miramichi River	Internet	understanding
women	prairie	rainfall	prejudices

A noun can be **singular** or **plural**. Usually the plural is formed by adding *s* or *es*, but there are many exceptions.

A noun can be the **subject** or the **object** in a sentence.

subject
|
The woman won.

object

Henri bought a pizza.

object

Steve carried it in a knapsack.

A **proper noun** names someone or something specific and begins with a capital letter. A **common noun** names someone or something in general and is not capitalized.

Proper nouns	Common nouns
Sammy Hundal	man
Nova Scotia	province
House of Commons	building

2. Pronouns

A **pronoun** takes the place of a noun.

noun   pronoun

David moaned when he saw how much work he had to do.

pronoun   noun

At first it only sniffed the grass, but soon the dog began to bark.

noun   pronoun

The server smiled happily. She had never received such a large tip before.

A pronoun must agree with the number, person, and gender of the noun it replaces.

third, singular, feminine   third, singular, feminine

Teresa learned to knit when she was young.

ON PERSON

The **first person** is the speaker. The **second person** is the person being spoken to. The **third person** is the person being spoken about.

• **I** (first person) am wearing a hat.

• **You** (second person) should put some sunscreen on.

• **She** (third person) is sitting in the shade to keep cool.

first, plural   first, plural

We said that the raft belonged to us.

For more information about pronouns, see pages 202–206.

Common Pronouns	Pronoun Number		
	Person	**Singular**	**Plural**
Subject Pronouns	first	I	we
	second	you	you
	third	he (masculine) she (feminine) it (neuter)	they
Object Pronouns	first	me	us
	second	you	you
	third	him (masculine) her (feminine) it (neuter)	them
Possessive Pronouns	first	my, mine	our, ours
	second	your, yours	your, yours
	third	his (masculine) her, hers (feminine) its (neuter)	their, theirs

3. Verbs

A **verb** expresses an action or a state of being. Some verbs describe a physical action: *run, break, explode.* Other verbs describe mental actions: *think, anticipate, wonder.* Still others express a state of being: *am, feel, appear, become.*

A verb must agree with its **subject**, which is either a noun or a pronoun. For more information about the kinds of subject/verb agreement, see pages 207–210.

Normally the subject of a verb does the action the verb describes. These are **active** verbs. But sometimes the verb is **passive**, and the subject receives the action.

Active: Kim *kicked* the ball.
Passive: The ball *was kicked* by Kim.

Your writing is more powerful when you use active verbs.

Helping verbs allow you to express different shades of meaning with other verbs.

helping verb   main verb

You can call Suzanne tomorrow.

helping verb   main verb

I should see her in the morning.

helping verb   main verb

She might tell me where she's been.

Some common helping verbs are *do, might, seem, would, can, could,* and all the forms of the verbs *to be* and *to have.*

Linking verbs join the subject of a sentence to an adjective or a noun in the predicate.

subject   linking verb   noun

The foothills became mountains.

Some common linking verbs are *look, sound, taste, smell, feel, seem, appear, become, grow, turn,* and all the forms of the verb *to be.*
For more about subjects and predicates, see page 194.

4. Adjectives
An **adjective** describes a noun or a pronoun.

adjectives   noun

We added some extra wood to the bonfire.

   pronoun adjective

It was dry and began to burn immediately.

You can use two or more adjectives together to describe one noun or pronoun.

She avoided the *thin, treacherous* ice that had formed where the river flowed quickly.

Articles are a special kind of adjective used to introduce a noun. There are only three articles: *a, an, the.*

The lynx took shelter in *a* tree with *an* old nest in it.

A patient photographer waited for *the* lynx to reappear.

5. Adverbs

An **adverb** tells about a verb, an adjective, or another adverb.

   adverb   verb

Tuan easily answered all the questions on the test.

     adverb adjective

That was an especially good baseball game.

           adverb adverb

Police responded to the emergency very quickly.

Many adverbs end in *ly*, which makes them easy to recognize.

Adverbs can also be used to compare two items.

          adverb   adverb

I hope they get here more quickly than they did last week.

          adverb

I'm sure Nellie will be here sooner than Jared.

6. Prepositions

A **preposition** is always followed by a noun or pronoun. Working together, these words create a **prepositional phrase**, which shows how the noun or pronoun relates to another word in the sentence.

prepositions related to nouns

She brought a glass of **water** from the kitchen.

preposition related to pronoun

He tasted some pasta, and then put some **salt** on **it**.

Common Prepositions				
about	because of	during	near	through
above	before	except	of	to
across	behind	for	off	toward
after	below	from	on	under
against	beneath	in	onto	underneath
along	beside	in front of	out	until
among	besides	inside	outside	up
around	between	instead of	over	upon
as	beyond	into	past	with
at	down	like	since	without

7. Conjunctions

A **conjunction** joins parts of a sentence together. The parts can be words, phrases, or clauses.

Some conjunctions join two or more equal parts.

noun   noun conjunction noun

I packed sunglasses, a sweater, **and** an umbrella so I would be ready for any kind of weather.

ON CONJUNCTIONS

Conjunctions that join two equal parts of a sentence:
and, but, for, or, so, yet

Conjunctions that show a special relationship between two ideas:

both...and
either...or
neither...nor
not only...but also
whether...or

Conjunctions that join a dependent clause to an independent clause:
after, although, as, as if, as though, because, before, if, since, so, than, that, though, unless, until, when, where, while

phrase conjunction phrase

There was a chance of rain **or** of snow.

clause   conjunction   clause

I thought I was ready, **but** the wind tore the umbrella from my hand.

Some conjunctions show a special relationship between two ideas.

conjunction   phrase   conjunction phrase

We could **either** go fishing in Roman's boat **or** stay here and fish off the dock.

conjunction   noun conjunction noun

Roman forgot **both** his fishing rod **and** his life jacket.

Some conjunctions join a dependent clause to an independent clause.

independent clause conjunction dependent clause

I can't come over **until** I finish my homework.

conjunction dependent clause   independent clause

Before I do my math, I will start my English assignment.

8. Interjections

An **interjection** is a word or phrase that expresses surprise or a strong emotion. Most interjections are short words, and they often appear at or near the beginning of a sentence.

interjection

Oh no! I think I left my wallet at home.

An interjection is followed by a punctuation mark, usually an exclamation mark. When an interjection appears in the middle of a sentence, use a comma before and after it to separate it from the rest of the sentence.

interjection

I looked and, thank goodness, I had shoved it in my backpack.

Punctuation

Punctuation marks make writing easier to read. They show where sentences, clauses, and phrases begin and end. They tell readers where to pause between pieces of information. They identify when someone says something, when a sentence is a question, and when a sentence expresses strong emotion. The most important punctuation marks are the ones shown in this box.

Symbol	What it looks like
period	That's the end.
question mark	What did you say?
exclamation mark	What a storm!
comma	The band has bells, whistles, and tambourines.
semicolon	That ended the session; we had to leave.
colon	These are the cars I like: Porsche, BMW, and Jaguar.
dash	We needed a break——so did our teachers.
apostrophe	That's my homework.
quotation marks	"And that's what I think," she said.
hyphen	I am a short-order cook.
parentheses	(I'll tell you later.)
ellipsis points	That's all for now...I hope.

Periods

A **period** is the stop sign placed at the end of most sentences.

It's a windy day.

Please help me get my kite in the air.

A period is sometimes used after the last letter of an abbreviation.

Mister = Mr.   Road = Rd.   Incorporated = Inc.
January = Jan.

ON QUESTION MARKS

You don't use a question mark when you write a question as part of a sentence. **We asked Jamal if he knew how many tickets he bought.**

Question Marks

A **question mark** is placed at the end of a question.

How many tickets did Jamal get?

Exclamation Marks

An **exclamation mark** is placed at the end of a sentence that expresses surprise or strong emotion, or gives a command.

I can't believe Zenaida won the raffle!

She had never felt so lucky!

You should buy a ticket next time!

An exclamation mark may follow an interjection (see also page 218).

Gross! That milk is sour.

Commas

A **comma** marks a brief pause in a sentence. It divides words, phrases, and clauses from one another, and joins words that work together as a unit. There are many rules for using commas, but if you are unsure, read the sentence aloud. If a pause feels natural, you probably need a comma. If a pause feels awkward, you probably don't need a comma. Here are some rules for using commas.

Commas separate words, phrases, or clauses in a series or list of three or more items.

Chickpeas, lemon juice, and olive oil are the main ingredients.

We learned how to sort the chickpeas, how to cook them, and how to grind them into a paste.

Put a comma between two or more adjectives that describe the same noun.

They struggled through the dense, thorny underbrush.

A comma can separate two independent clauses that are joined by a conjunction. However, it often is left out, especially when the clauses are very short.

I know how to parachute, but every jump makes me a bit nervous.

I jumped and my parachute opened.

A comma separates an introductory phrase or word from the rest of the sentence.

After looking in two bookstores, Tang Yu decided to try the library.

Unfortunately, the library was closed.

Commas are used to set off a word or comment that interrupts a sentence but does not add essential information to the main idea of the sentence.

Hard work, Marisa knew, would be one way of solving the problem.

The blazing heat, which Miguel loved, dried up the crops.

Peter's watch, which his father had given him, was broken.

A comma must *not* separate a clause from the rest of the sentence if that clause gives essential information about the main ideas of the sentence.

The blazing heat that lasted all of August dried up the crops.

The watch that Peter wanted cost more than the old one.

Use a comma, or commas, around a noun when you address someone directly in your writing.

Jason, tell us why you are the best candidate.

I ask you, fellow students, to support me on election day.

A comma, or commas, separates dialogue from the rest of a sentence.

"I read about it yesterday," he continued, "and I took some notes."

For more about how to punctuate dialogue, see page 182.

Semicolons

A **semicolon**, like a comma, marks a pause in a sentence. A semicolon joins two independent clauses and can take the place of these conjunctions: *and, but, for, or, so, yet.*

independent clause
|
On Tuesday, she has band practice at lunch and a yearbook meeting after school; it will be a busy day.

independent clause

Colons

A **colon** marks a strong break in a sentence. It is often used to introduce a list. Make sure that whatever goes before the colon is a complete sentence: never use a colon after a sentence fragment.

Bashir demonstrated the following karate techniques: front kick, side kick, lunge punch, reverse punch, upper block, and down block.

A colon can also be used to introduce a complete sentence that explains, expands upon, or illustrates the sentence before the colon.

My cat hates to eat directly from her bowl: she carries her food into the living room and eats it there.

Dashes
Dashes are used in pairs to surround a thought that interrupts the flow of a sentence.

Teresa, Julie, and Kirstin——who were new to the area——walked into town to watch a movie at the theatre.

A dash can also be used to show a change in thought or tone within a sentence.

Every Saturday night we go to a movie or hang out at the mall——there's nothing else to do around here.

Apostrophes
An **apostrophe** is used to create the possessive form of nouns. It also takes the place of missing letters in contractions.

possessive noun

This is his sister's Web site.

contraction

He can't go near it.

Quotation Marks
Quotation marks are used in dialogue (see page 181).

Use quotation marks around the titles of short stories, poems, magazine articles, or chapters within a book.

I liked the poem "Trombone Solo" best.

Hyphens

A **hyphen** joins two or more words to show they function as a single word.

> She is the best-loved parrot in the pet shop.

Parentheses

Parentheses surround a word or an idea that adds information to a sentence.

> Heather (a doctor) and Simone (the owner of a local business) both spoke at the public meeting.

> Zach told me (but I didn't believe him) that the snake had escaped from its cage.

Dashes can be used instead of parentheses to set off a word or comment within a sentence, but dashes give the extra information more importance.

Ellipsis Points

Usually an **ellipsis** (...) shows that words have been left out of a quotation.

> **Full statement**: This movie has everything—solid acting, an excellent story, spectacular scenery, and a thoughtful message. It is packed with action and will keep you on the edge of your seat.

> **Quotation with an ellipsis**: This movie...will keep you on the edge of your seat.

In dialogue, ellipsis points indicate an incomplete thought.

> Looking puzzled, Nikki said, "She walked right past me...without saying hello...without even looking at me. She just...." (The period after the last ellipsis shows that the sentence has ended.)

To learn about punctuating dialogue, see page 182.

We use standard spelling to make communication easier. Standard spelling allows people to read and understand what you have written. Non-standard spelling may make your reader spend more time thinking about your spelling than thinking about the opinions and ideas in your writing.

When is correct spelling really important? Spelling is most important in a piece of writing that you want other people to read. When you are writing for yourself or writing a first draft of something, spelling is not as important, as long as you know what you mean.

Tips for Improving Your Spelling

One way to improve your spelling is to look for spelling patterns. There are three common sets of spelling patterns in English.

Sound Patterns: Look for words, or parts of words, that sound alike: *ship, shore, shampoo; bread, head.*

Meaning Patterns: Look for words that share similar or related meanings: *two, twice, twins; visible, vision, visual.* These are sometime called word families.

Function Patterns: Look for words that are the same part of speech. For example, you add **ed** to most verbs to make the past tense, no matter how the ending is pronounced: *load**ed**, call**ed**, jump**ed**.*

If there is a word that you always have trouble spelling, see if it fits a spelling pattern that will help you remember the correct spelling.

Keep a list of the words you misspell. Look them up in a dictionary and write them correctly in an alphabetical list. Then use your list for reference when you are writing. If you put a check mark beside a word in your list each time you find that you've spelled it correctly without looking it up, you'll have a record of how your spelling is improving.

TECHNOLOGY TIP

Computer spell checkers have made it easier to pick up obvious spelling errors that may slip by when you proofread your writing. But a spell checker doesn't know when you've used **there** instead of **their**, or **right** instead of **write**.

Make up your own memory aids. Sentences, poems, or phrases about spelling patterns, and odd ways of pronouncing words, can help you remember how to spell difficult words. See the rhyme about "i before e" in the margin.

If you aren't sure how to spell a word, follow these steps.

1. Think about the way the word looks. Write it down the way you think it might be spelled. If it doesn't look right, try again.
2. Look up your best version of the word in the dictionary. Some sounds can be spelled in more than one way. If you can't find a word in a dictionary, there may be a different way to spell one of the sounds in the word. See the chart below.

COMMONLY MISSPELLED WORDS

absence
accidentally
accurate
achievement
actual
among
ancient
angle
answer
anxious
arctic
argument
association
audience
awkward
believe
brought
business
busy
calendar
cannot

Sound (consonants)	Different Spellings
f	fish, physical
sk	skip, scare, school
s	soft, civil, psychology
sh	ship, chef
k	kick, candy, chemistry, quiche
r	roof, wrinkle
n	now, knife, gnome, pneumonia, mnemonic

Sound (vowels)	Different Spellings
a (as in cave)	trace, train, day
e (as in me)	these, team, see, key
o (as in go)	bone, coat, toe, low

3. When you have found the word in the dictionary, check the pronunciation and read the definitions. Knowing more about the word may help you remember it.
4. Practice spelling the word: look at it spelled correctly, and then cover it up and write it down. Check to see if you spelled it correctly.

ceiling
cemetery
centre
certain
changeable
climb
colour
commercial
committed
committee
concerning
congratulate
conscience
cooperate
criticize
definition
dependent
develop
disappear
doubt
early
eight
embarrass
enough
especially
essential
exaggerate
excellent
famous
favourite
February
foreign
fortunate
forty
fourth
friend
generally
geography
government
guarantee

Confusing Words

There are many words that sound the same but are different in spelling and meaning. When you proofread your work, keep this in mind and make sure you've chosen the correct word. When in doubt, check the word in a dictionary.

a lot (**of**)—a phrase meaning *much, many,* or *often: We have a lot of time. The library has a lot of books. We visit each other a lot.*
alot—an incorrect spelling of *a lot.*

accept—a verb meaning *to receive: I accepted the invitation.*
except—a preposition meaning *other than: Everyone came, except Jacques.*

advice—a noun meaning *an opinion about something: Her advice was to get a study partner.*
advise—a verb meaning *to give advice to: My teacher advised me to study harder.*

affect—a verb meaning *to influence: The loss of their best player badly affected the team's performance.*
effect—a noun meaning *a result: A flood may be one effect of all this rain.*

aloud—an adverb meaning *out loud: Bryan read the story aloud to his little sister.*
allowed—a verb meaning *to permit: Are you allowed to drive your mother's car?*

beside—a preposition meaning *by the side of: She sat beside me.*
besides—an adverb or preposition meaning *in addition to: No one understands Pierre besides me.*

choose—a verb in the present tense meaning *to make a choice: Today, I choose to quit the team.*
chose—the same verb in the past tense: *A year ago, I chose to join the team.*

guess
half
hazardous
headache
height
honour
humorous
illustrate
immediately
impatient
importance
instance
instead
intelligence
island
jewellery
journal
label
laboratory
language
laugh
likable
literature
mathematics
meant
measure
minute
mysterious
naturally
necessary
neither
nickel
ninety
noisy
noticeable
nuclear
occasionally
occur
often
opinion

complement—a verb meaning *goes well with*: *That colour complements your eyes.*

compliment—a noun meaning *an expression of praise*: *The singer received many compliments for her fine performance.*

could have—a verb form suggesting a failed chance: *I could have gone, if I had had money.*

could of—an incorrect use of the verb form *could have.*

it's—the contraction of *it is*: *It's hard to say goodbye to a friend.*

its—the possessive form of *it*: *Fido is too big for its owner.*

knew—a verb in the past tense meaning *to have knowledge of*: *I knew the answer.*

new—an adjective meaning *the opposite of old*: *Are there any new movies out?*

later—an adjective or adverb meaning *after some time*: *He got home later than his sister.*

latter—an adjective meaning *the second of two*: *The latter of his two excuses was more believable.*

loose—an adjective meaning *untied* or *free*: *Her belt was loose.*

lose—a verb meaning *to misplace* or *fail to win*: *Don't lose your hat! You will lose this game if you don't concentrate harder.*

passed—a verb in the past tense meaning *to go by*: *The garbage truck passed our house.*

past—a word meaning *the time before the present, finished,* or *farther than*: *She had a troubled past. The past president walked past the podium.*

quiet—an adjective meaning *silent*: *He was so quiet; he rarely spoke.*

quite—an adverb meaning *very, really,* or *completely*: *The trees are quite lovely.*

than—a conjunction used to make a comparison: *A grapefruit is bigger than a lemon.*

then—an adverb meaning *immediately afterward*: *Gene did his homework, and then he read a book.*

opposite
paragraph
particularly
people
persuade
piece
possess
possible
precious
preferred
prejudice
presence
privilege
procedure
realize
receive
rhyme
rhythm
scene
science
separate
several
sincerely
specific
straight
succeed
surrounded
technique
temperature
thorough
though
thought
truly
unique
usable
useful
valuable
Wednesday
weird
women

their—the possessive form of *they*: *Many of their friends have left.*

there—an adverb identifying place: *Everyone goes there to shop.*

they're—the contraction of *they are*: *They're going to stay in Copelin.*

threw—a verb in the past tense meaning *to throw*: *She threw the ball to first base.*

through—a preposition meaning *from end to end*: *She tossed the ball through the goal posts.*

to—a preposition meaning *in the direction of, as far as*, or *along with*: *Owen went to school.*

too—an adverb meaning *also, as well as*, or *very*: *It is too cold to go swimming.*

two—the number: *The store was over two miles away.*

wear—a verb meaning *to have on the body*: *Carlos refused to wear his new suit.*

where—a word meaning *place*: *Where did you go? We went to the store where Jordan works.*

who's—the contraction of *who is* or *who has*: *Who's going camping this summer?*

whose—the possessive form of *who*: *Sasha, whose tent we used last summer, has moved away.*

your—the possessive form of *you*: *Please read your geography textbook.*

you're—the contraction for *you are*: *You're going to learn about the water table.*

we're—the contraction for *we are*: *We're all going to the basketball game.*

were—a form of the verb *to be*: *We were inspired by the poem "Foul Shot."*

weather—a noun meaning *the climate conditions outside*: *The summer brings warm and sunny weather.*

whether—a conjunction meaning *if*: *He didn't know whether to stay or to leave.*

Oral and Visual Communication Power Tools

Have you ever felt like yawning while listening to someone speak? Have you ever wondered if your audience felt that way while you were speaking? If so, the strategies in this section can help you and your classmates become more effective communicators.

You use oral and visual communication tools to understand and explain the world around you. These tools help you to make sense of conversations, classroom presentations, TV news, movies, and advertising, and they help you communicate your ideas more effectively.

Reprinted with special permission of King Features Syndicate.

Oral Communication

GROUP DISCUSSIONS

These are some of the benefits of class and small-group discussions.
- Speaking with other people introduces you to new ideas and new ways of thinking about things.
- You may understand your own ideas better after you have explained and defended them to others.
- You sharpen your critical-thinking skills by comparing your ideas with those of other people.
- Talking over a problem with other people can help you to find new solutions.
- A group of people working together to brainstorm ideas will come up with many more ideas than will one person working alone.

For longer group discussion projects, each group member should take one of the roles listed below. You may not need all of these roles for each project.
- leader (to keep discussions on track)
- recorder (to take notes)
- readers (to read things aloud)
- timekeeper (to keep track of the time)
- reporter (to report back to the whole class)

Here are some tips to help you make group discussions work well.
- Be prepared. Before you meet, do the reading, make notes, list questions you might ask, and think about what you want to say.
- Keep the conversation focused on the topic.
- Keep an open mind. There often is no one right answer: instead, there may be many different ways of looking at a topic.
- Encourage all group members to take part in the discussion and to ask questions about anything they don't understand.

- Respect everyone in the group.
- Use only polite language when disagreeing with others.
- Listen politely to others, without interrupting them.
- Don't take over the discussion.

YOUR TURN

You will probably have many opportunities to be involved in class and small-group discussions. Always keep in mind the above tips for good group discussions. If you would like to try a group discussion but need a topic, here are a few to choose from.

Discuss non-fiction in a group: Work together to prepare a summary of the main points.

Discuss poetry in a group: Prepare three questions about a poem and discuss possible answers to the questions. Or decide on the three most important words in the poem.

Discuss a short story in a group: Choose your favourite part of the story and explain your choice to the group. Or choose three important quotations from the story, read them to the group, and explain their importance.

GOOD LISTENING SKILLS

Are you a good listener? Evaluate your listening skills by answering these questions.
- Do I think of listening to someone as a chance to learn?
- Do I look at the person who is speaking?
- Do I pay attention, without letting my mind wander?
- Do I remember the important points a speaker makes?
- Do I listen to what a speaker says before I judge the speaker and his or her ideas?
- Do I listen patiently, without interrupting the speaker?
- Do I listen to what others say and try to add to their ideas?
- Do I pay attention to the speaker's facial expressions and hand gestures while he or she is speaking?

If you said yes to five or more of these questions, you are well on your way to being a good listener. Listening is a skill that you can improve with effort and practice. Here are some strategies.

Listening Skills for Group Discussions Good listeners contribute to group discussions in these ways.

- They encourage the person who is speaking by looking at the speaker and by paying attention.
- They summarize what someone has said and try to add to it.
- They ask questions when they don't understand something.
- They jot down ideas and questions to keep track of what is being said and refer to their notes when they speak.

Listening to Make Notes When you listen in class, or during interviews, or while watching a film or TV show, you may want to make notes about what you hear. Listening and taking notes at the same time is a real challenge. Below are some ideas.

- Before the person begins to speak, think about why you are listening and what you hope to learn from what is being said.
- Be selective—don't try to write down every point. Note key words and fill in the details later.
- Watch for the speaker's hand gestures and facial expressions. Listen for signal words, like *most important* or *in addition,* to give you clues to the main points of the presentation.
- Notice how the speaker has organized the material and follow the same pattern in your note-taking. Does the speaker always ask a question to introduce a new idea? Does the speaker summarize each main point?
- When the speaker has finished, go over your notes and add any details you may have missed.

For more on note-taking, see the Tutorial on page 64.

YOUR TURN

In a group discussion, be the recorder for the group and take notes. Follow the tips given above, and then ask your group to evaluate your notes. Did you include all the important points? Did you leave out anything important?

To make a successful presentation, you must be well prepared. Here are some things to keep in mind as you prepare a presentation.

Your Purpose and Your Audience As you begin to work on your presentation, answer these questions.

- Why am I giving this presentation?
- Who is my audience?
- Do I want to inform my audience, entertain my audience, or persuade them of something?

For more about audience and purpose, see page 151.

The way you write your presentation will depend on your audience. For your classmates, you can use everyday language, as long as you avoid slang or repetitive expressions.

> **Not Recommended**: "Like, the whole place was just awesome!"
> **Improved**: "The whole exhibit was impressive! There were virtual reality games, and outside there was a wall you could actually climb!"

For an adult audience, such as a group of teachers and parents, you should use more formal language. Have an adult read over or listen to your presentation to make sure the language is right for your audience.

For more information on writing, see pages 136–161 and 177–193.

How to Write Your Presentation You use the same skills to write a presentation as you do to write any other assignment. However, you may find some of these tips useful for preparing a presentation.

- You can use notes instead of a complete script to make a presentation. Make your notes on index cards, in large, clear writing, so you can read them easily. Put one main point with supporting details on each card. Then number the cards in order.
- If you prefer to work with a complete script, write your presentation out in full. Underline or highlight words you want to emphasize, and mark pauses. Number the pages in order.

- Use your script or notes to help you organize the use of visuals, sound effects, or other special elements. Write cues in the margins of your notes, in a second colour, to remind you about what to do.
- Use language that comes naturally to you, and keep your sentences fairly short and easy to read. Explain any terms you think your audience may not know.
- Don't start by saying "My topic is…." Look at Writing Powerful Leads on page 178 for some other suggestions for opening an essay or report. These will also work well for a presentation.
- Tell your audience exactly what the purpose or main point of your presentation is.
- Repeat your main point throughout your presentation.
- Help your audience to follow your ideas. Use transition words such as *first, second, therefore, in addition,* and *finally*. For more information about transition words, see page 147.
- Do something unexpected. Have some fun with your presentation. You could
  - wear a simple costume, such as a hat or an unusual jacket. Be sure to choose a costume related to the topic of your presentation.
  - give your presentation while playing the role of an appropriate character. For example, become one of the Crash Test Dummies to talk about music, or take on the role of a flood survivor to talk about the Red River or the Saguenay River floods.
  - try organizing your presentation as a guided tour, a news report, or a game show.
- Provide a strong conclusion. At the end of your presentation, remind your audience of your main points and sum up your message in a way that people will remember. You might use a good quotation or a personal story. For example, here is one way you might end a presentation about dogs.

I said at the beginning of my presentation that dogs are amazing animals. I agree with Gilda Radner when she says that "they give unconditional love. For me they are the role model of being alive." I hope you agree!"

Using Visuals and Props A short video clip, a photograph, or an object related to your topic can help you to capture the attention of your audience. Be sure to follow these tips.

- All visuals and props must *add* something to your presentation. They should not be filler or a distraction.
- Too many visuals are worse than none; don't confuse your audience or yourself!
- Set up the equipment you need before you start to speak. Make sure that it works and that you know how to run it.
- Rehearse your presentation with your visuals and props so you are comfortable with them.

Rehearsing A well-prepared presentation can still come across as confusing or disorganized if the presenters have not rehearsed. This is a very important step.

- Read your presentation out loud several times. Rewrite any sentences that make you stumble. Write notes to remind yourself about how to read specific sentences.
- Practice speaking in a strong, steady, clear voice. Audiotape or videotape your rehearsal so you can hear and see yourself, and look for ways to improve your presentation style.

Timing For most presentations, you are given a specific time limit. The length of time you have will limit how much information you can include in your presentation. When you rehearse your presentation, make sure you time it.

- If your presentation is too long, cut out the least important material and try again. Rehearse, revise, and rehearse again.
- Do not try to make your presentation shorter by speaking more quickly. Your audience cannot listen more quickly!

Beating the Jitters Don't worry—most people get nervous! Here are some tips to help you work with your nervous energy.

- What is the best way to beat the jitters? Know your presentation and your topic well. Be prepared!
- Before your presentation, find a quiet place where you can relax and take a few deep breaths. Or just close your eyes for a moment and breathe deeply.
- Use gentle stretching exercises to help you relax.

- Use your nervous energy to help you add energy during your presentation.
- Your nervousness will likely decrease as you speak, especially if you feel confident about your presentation.

Speaking Keep these tips in mind as you speak to your audience.
- Wait for the audience to be quiet before you start.
- Speak steadily in a loud, clear voice. Speak a little more loudly than you think you have to and pronounce each word clearly.
- Look up at your audience as much as possible.
- Keep both feet on the ground and try not to shuffle. Keep your hands still unless you are making an intentional gesture.
- Make your voice expressive, as you would when talking about something interesting with a friend. Changes in the volume and speed of your speaking voice can add emphasis and excitement to your presentation.

Answering Questions Give your audience time at the end of the presentation to ask questions.
- Listen carefully to each question. If you don't understand, ask the person to repeat the question.
- Take a moment to think about your answer, and then give as direct an answer as possible. When you don't know the answer, say so. Never make up an answer!

YOUR TURN

The next time you prepare a presentation, follow the suggestions given on pages 234–235, and keep a journal about what you do each day as you work on the presentation. Then write about how you felt as you gave the presentation. When the presentation is complete, look over your journal and make suggestions about what you might do differently next time to improve your work.

An **interview** is a conversation in which one person—the interviewer—asks questions to learn something from another person —the interviewee. People in the media frequently interview politicians, business and technical experts, and celebrities. Employers interview possible employees. You can use interviews when you do research for assignments. Here are some tips to help you become a good interviewer.

Before the Interview Make sure you have a clear purpose for the interview. Then choose the right person to interview—someone who has the information you need. Then follow these steps.

- Do your homework. Find out as much as you can about the person and your topic, so you can ask good questions.
- Write a list of questions. The W5 + H questions (see page 75) are good questions to start with because they demand thoughtful answers.
- Keep your list of questions short, and estimate how long the interview will take. Allow time for questions that occur to you during the interview.
- Prepare your final list of questions, leaving space after each question to take notes about the answer.
- Set up the interview. Contact the person and explain the purpose of the interview. Let the person know what kinds of questions you'll ask and how long the interview will take. Suggest a time and place to meet, or allow the interviewee to choose the time and place.
- Decide how to record the interview. You should always take handwritten notes, but you might also use a tape recorder or video camera. Ask permission before you record an interview. Some people will refuse to be recorded. If you do use a tape recorder or video camera, make sure you know how to use it.
- Listen to interviews on radio or watch some on TV to see how the interviews are conducted.

During the Interview Follow these tips for conducting a lively interview.

- Arrive on time, or be early if you have equipment to set up. Don't waste your interviewee's time!
- Start with a friendly question to make the interviewee feel comfortable. For example, if you are interviewing an astronomer, you might start with this question: "What first got you interested in astronomy?"
- Show that you are interested in what the person says. Nod your head to show you understand. Make eye contact when you ask a question and lean forward slightly to show you are listening.
- Listen carefully. Don't be so worried about what you're going to ask next that you miss the answers. If you need time to write notes during the interview, ask the interviewee to pause for a moment, rather than miss what is said.
- Improvise. If you think of a good question that's not on your list, ask it. If you don't understand something, ask politely for more information or another example. You can always go back to your prepared questions later.
- Don't talk too much or show off about how much *you* know. Use the interview to learn about what the *other* person knows.

After the Interview Do the following as soon as possible after the interview is over.

- Send a thank-you note to the person you interviewed.
- Review your notes and any recording made during the interview. Make notes about anything you missed and add information needed to explain the notes you did make.

YOUR TURN

Practice your interviewing skills with a classmate. Choose a topic your partner knows well, and interview him or her on that topic. Then switch roles: this time your partner will interview you.

AUDIOTAPING

You can use audiotaping to make a permanent record of an interview, an oral presentation, or a radio advertisement.

Before you begin audiotaping, think about what you are recording. How many people will be speaking? Will you be able to work with one microphone, or will you need more than one? Will your equipment allow you to use more than one microphone?

Here are some general tips for making a successful audiotape.

- Make sure your equipment is ready, you have batteries, and you know how to use the equipment.
- Put one person in charge of operating the tape recorder.
- Make a test recording to check the microphone and the recording level.
- Begin the recording session by giving the date, the names of the people involved, and the title of the project. Make sure you label the tape, too.
- Speak clearly at a steady pace, and use variety in your speaking voice. If your voice always sounds the same, your audience will have difficulty listening to you.
- If you are speaking from a script, rehearse with the script until you can speak your lines easily and naturally.
- If your finished tape is too long, choose the most important passages and rerecord them to produce the "edited highlights" of your recording session.

YOUR TURN

With a partner or a small group, record a Reader's Theatre presentation of the poem "Snow Shadows," on page 39. Prepare for the recording by practicing different ways of reading the poem to construct different interpretations. Create a unique sound picture of the poem. Play your tape for an audience. Did you succeed in creating the effect you intended?

Visual Communication

THE ROLE OF THE MASS MEDIA

The mass media include television, movies, music videos, video games, newspapers, magazines, chat lines on the Internet, T-shirts with logos, and even lunch bags with images from popular cartoons and movies. Media images are so much a part of our lives that we often don't pay much attention to them. However, these images carry messages, which we often accept without a lot of thought. If you learn to notice the messages, you can decide for yourself if you agree with them or not.

Use this survey to see what role the media play in your life.

Media Survey

1. a) How much time do you spend each week watching TV?
      Watching videos?
      Listening to CDs and tapes?
      Listening to the radio?
      Using the Internet?
      Reading newspapers or magazines?
      Playing computer games?
   b) Which of these activities is your favourite? Why?

2. What are your three favourite TV shows? Why do you like them?

3. a) Describe your favourite male and female characters on TV.
   b) What do these two TV characters have in common? How are they different?

4. a) What is your favourite type of music and who is your favourite performer?
   b) How did you first hear about this performer?

5. a) If you won a $5 000 shopping spree, where would you spend the money? What would you buy?
   b) How did you find out about these stores and these products?

YOUR TURN

Complete the media survey yourself and have at least five other people complete it. Summarize your findings and report them to the class as a brief documentary or news story on the role of the media in people's lives.

READING MEDIA MESSAGES

Some media messages are obvious. We know an ad for jeans is telling us to buy them. But that ad may also be telling us that being "beautiful" means being slim and tall, with well-developed muscles.

All media products, or "media texts," carry indirect messages about what to expect of people based on things like their appearance, age, skin colour, and degree of wealth. These messages also influence our goals and our ideas about success.

On the next page are some questions you can ask about a media text to help you analyze its indirect messages. Use these questions when watching a TV show, movie, or music video, or when reading a magazine.

Reading Indirect Media Messages

What Do You See? (The Media Text)

What "story" does the media text tell? Is it part of a larger story?

Does the story follow a pattern or a formula you recognize?

Who are the people in the media text? Are they realistic? Are they stereotypes?

What are the people doing? Do they behave in predictable ways?

If you could retell the story, what would you have the people do?

What does the story suggest is important?

Who Is Watching? (The Audience)

What do you like or dislike about the media text?

Who do you think is the intended audience for the media text?

What part of the media text do you think appeals most to the audience?

Do you see yourself reflected in any part of the media text? Why or why not?

What might other people think about this media text? Think of men versus women, teens versus adults, and the reactions of people from different cultural backgrounds.

Who Made What You See? (The Production)

Who created the media text?

What production techniques were used to create the media text?

How could you create a similar media text?

How is the media text sold or distributed to the public?

How much does the media text cost? What do you think its actual value might be?

Who will make money from the media text? How will that money likely be used?

YOUR TURN

Choose two media texts that tell a similar story using different media. For example, you might choose a television ad and a short story or movie featuring a family vacation. Use the above questionnaire to help you analyze and compare the two media texts. Begin by jotting down what you think of each media text when you first see it. Then use the questions above to analyze both media texts. Read over your answers and note the similarities and differences in the indirect messages the two media texts carry. Finally, ask yourself if your opinion of the media texts changed at all as you completed this activity.

Photographs appear in books, magazines, newspapers, and many other places. They may be used to add interest to a story or to provide information. Some photographs are created as artwork, to be enjoyed or appreciated much like a painting. Here are some terms you can use when talking about photographs.

Subject: the main focus or object in a photograph; what the photograph is about.

Frame: the edges of a photograph. A photographer uses the frame to include or leave out details in a photograph.

Lighting: the amount and kind of light visible in a photograph. Lighting may be artificial or natural, bright or soft, and there may be contrast between areas of brightness and shadow. The lighting has a strong effect on a photograph's mood or feeling.

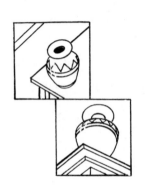

Camera Angle: the point of view of a photograph. A photographer may look down from a high angle, up from a low angle, or straight at a subject. The camera angle also has a strong effect on the mood or feeling of a photograph.

The photographer uses the frame, lighting, and camera angles, as well as other techniques, to create a unique picture that tells the audience something about the subject. The following questions will help you think about and discuss what individual photographs say about their subjects.

- If you could be a part of the scene in the photograph, where would you want to be? Why?
- Where does the photograph appear? Are there other pictures with it? What pictures appear before or after it? How do the photographs relate to one another?
- Is there a caption? If so, what does it say? Is there other text around the picture? If so, what does it say? How does the caption or the surrounding text affect the way you interpret the photograph?

- Has the photographer included anything within the frame of the photograph that you might have left out? Can you imaging anything you might have chosen to include? Why do you think the photographer chose to include or leave out these things?
- What do you think is the purpose of the photograph? Was it created to entertain, to inform, or to persuade a viewer of something? Explain your answer, referring to details in the photograph.

YOUR TURN

Look at the photograph reproduced here. Use the questions above as the starting point for a discussion about this photograph with a partner or small group. Choose photographs from your personal collections or from magazines and newspapers and prepare a photo essay that builds on and reflects the meaning of this photograph.

VIEWING A FILM

Films, or movies, tell stories in much the same way as short stories or novels do. Some films might also be compared to poems, full of imagery that appeals to the senses. Films use many of the same techniques as photographs, but add sound and motion. You can use the suggestions found on page 244 for Viewing a Photograph to examine the camera techniques used in films. In addition, here are some terms you can use to talk about specific moments or scenes in a film.

Shot: all the action recorded in one run of the camera, without interruption or change in point of view. In a car chase, one shot might show the driver's face through the windshield. For more about types of shots, see page 251.

Cut: the end of a shot; the change from one shot to another, which may be sudden, or more gradual as in a fade or dissolve.

Scene: a series of shots all related to one part of an event. In a car chase, one scene might be the part of a car chase that takes place on one street.

Sequence: a series of scenes all related to one topic or event, with a clear beginning and ending. For example, many action films have a car-chase sequence.

You can use the following sets of questions to guide your thoughts when you review or assess a film. You need not answer all of these questions for each film. Simply choose the questions that focus on the most important parts of each film.

Your Personal Response
- Did I enjoy the film?
- Did the film remind me of anything in my own life or of any other films I have seen?
- What were my favourite and least favourite moments in the film?
- What did I think or feel about the film a day or two after seeing it?

Technical Elements (sound, music, lighting, camera angles and movement, special effects, costumes, sets)
- What did I notice about each of these elements?
- Did anything stand out as well done or poorly done?
- Did anything about the technical elements not seem to fit with the rest of the film?

Characters
- Did the characters seem like real people?
- Did I care about them?
- Were the characters' actions easy to predict or surprising?

Acting
- Did the speech or actions of any of the characters seem forced or unnatural?
- Did the characters come alive?

continued on next page

Credibility
- Did the actions and events in the film seem as if they could really happen?
- If the film had an imaginative setting, such as a science fiction film or an animated film, did the actions and events make sense within the reality of the film?
- Did anything that happened in the film seem out of place?

Overall Theme or Subject
- What was the film about?
- Did the film say anything interesting about people or the way they behave?

If you have been asked to write a film review, you could use the following format as a guide.

Paragraph 1: Identify the name of the film, the director, the screenwriter, and the main actors involved. You might also include a brief comment about your opinion of the film.

Paragraph 2: Give a brief summary of the events in the film, a brief description of the characters involved, and perhaps some information about the setting. You might also include a short statement summarizing the theme or message of the film, but be very careful not to give away the ending of the film.

Paragraph 3: Compare the film to related films, such as ones on a similar theme, or ones with the same actors, director, or writer. If the film is based on a story, novel, or play, compare the film to the original, if possible.

Paragraph 4: Give your opinion on the quality of the film, whether it was good or bad. Support your opinion with examples from the film. You could end your review with a recommendation about whether to see the film at a theatre, wait to see it on video, or not see it at all.

VIEWING A TELEVISION SHOW

Television is the most popular form of mass media. On network television, the money needed to produce the shows is earned by selling advertising time. So the primary job of any successful television program is to attract an audience that is appropriate for the show's advertisers.

Television shows use many of the same production techniques as films. You can respond to many television shows, especially TV movies, using the same questions provided for Viewing a Film on page 245. However, because audience is so important for all television shows, you should also identify and think about the target audience for a TV show.

Target Audience

• Who are the main characters in the TV show? Describe each character's age, gender, race, job, education, and income.
• Who do you think is most likely to watch this show? Is it a popular show?
• What advertisements are run during the show? Describe the products and who is most likely to buy or use them.
• Based on your answers to the above questions, who is the target audience for this show? Are you part of it?

Many television shows seem to be a reflection of reality. The people and places in these shows may seem very familiar to you from your daily life. However, television shows are carefully created to appeal to specific audiences and to tell specific stories. You can use a chart like the following to do a reality check for a specific television show, or for a type or genre of television show.

Reality Check

Title or Type of Show: _____

Common Images From Show	Similar Scenes From Real Life	Comparison of TV and Real Life
• An attractive, witty host leads a conversation.	• We all get together at lunch to talk; no one really leads the conversation.	• TV show is more controlled, better organized.
• Guests always have interesting stories to tell.	• Sometimes no one has anything really interesting to say.	• You almost never see boring people on talk shows.

YOUR TURN

Use a chart like the one above to compare your favourite television show, or your favourite type of show, to real life. You may have to do some research to fill in the "Similar Scenes From Real Life" column. Then answer this question: How well does television reflect reality? Support your answer with examples from your chart.

POSTERS AND ADS

Posters and print ads can be used to advertise products or services, to give information about an event, or to promote an idea. Effective posters grab your attention and hold it long enough to deliver a message. Ask yourself the questions on the next page.

- What catches my eye and holds my attention?
- Do I like posters with more words, or more pictures?
- What are my favourite slogans? Do they have anything in common?

As you plan and create your own poster or print ad, try to use techniques that have worked well in the ads and posters you like. Your answers to the following questions should help with planning an effective poster.

- What is my subject? What do I want to say about it?
- Who is my target audience? What are their special interests?
- What words and/or images are associated with my subject?

Make sure you give your poster a strong centre of attention—one central word, phrase, or picture that will grab the attention of your audience. If you include pictures of people, choose models who will appeal to your target audience. For example, you would probably use different models in a poster about road safety for an elementary school audience than you would for a secondary school audience. As you select models, think about their age, gender, and race. Finally, think about the colours and objects you associate with your subject, and choose the ones that will create the mood or feeling you want your poster to convey.

YOUR TURN

Working alone or with a partner, plan and create a rough draft for a poster promoting an event, a club, or a class at your school. Use the questions above to help you plan your work.

**LONG TRACKING SHOT
PAULINE ON STANLEY
APPROACHING CORRAL**

**MEDIUM SHOT
PAULINE RIDES HORSE
INTO CORRAL**

**HIGH ANGLE
PAULINE BRUSHES STANLEY**

CLOSE UP   PAULINE SPEAKS

A storyboard is a series of sketches with captions that are used to plan a video production. The sketches show the type of camera shots and what will be visible in each shot. The captions include the dialogue or script, if any, plus any extra directions for lighting, shot type, camera angles, music, voice overs (VO), or sound effects (SFX).

Here are some terms that you may find useful.

Normal or Straight Angle: the camera looks straight at the subject.

High Angle: the camera looks down on the subject.

Low Angle: the camera looks up at the subject.

Close Up (CU): the camera is very close to the subject. You would see only the head and shoulders of a person.

Long Shot (LS): the camera is a long way from the subject. You would see all of a person plus some surrounding scenery.

Medium Shot (MS): the camera is halfway between a CU and an LS. You would see the head and most of the body of a person.

Tracking or Follow Shot: the camera follows along with the action of the subject, for example, following a character who is running.

Point of View (POV): the camera shows what a character would see from his or her point of view. For example, a crowd shot from a young child's point of view would show mostly legs and feet.

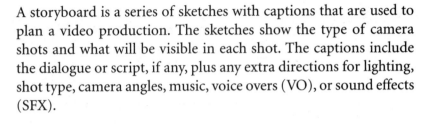

YOUR TURN

Finish the incomplete storyboard above for the beginning of "Ride to the Hill," page 42. Begin by writing in your notebook the directions for the shots already sketched here. Then add sketches and directions for at least three or four more shots.

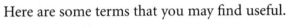

MAKING YOUR OWN VIDEO

Before you begin making your own video, decide what type of video you want to make. Will it be a documentary? A news show? A commercial? A talk show? Watch similar shows on TV, and pay attention to the sets, to how long each shot lasts, to the lighting and sound, to any special effects, and to where the people stand or move. Then write a script and prepare a detailed storyboard.

The following tips should help you create a successful video.
- Assign someone to fill each of these roles: director, actors, camera operator, sound technician.
- Rehearse each scene before you begin to shoot. Revise the directions in the script or storyboard for any shot or scene that does not work.
- Make sure the camera is loaded with film, the batteries are charged, and there are no distracting background noises.
- Use a tripod to keep the camera steady. Use a variety of camera angles and distances to add interest.
- Keep all props, costumes, and sets until you have viewed the video. You may need to reshoot some scenes.

As you work on your video, pause at key stages, such as after you have completed your storyboard, after you have rehearsed the script, and after you have filmed half of your production, to assess your progress. Do not wait until the end, because it may be too late at that point to reshoot or revise your production.

YOUR TURN

Plan a short documentary video about what it is like to be a student at your school. Prepare a storyboard of possible shots; then shoot no more than three minutes of tape. Use a variety of camera angles and shots. Then edit your production down to one minute, using either editing equipment or two VCRs.

Index

ACKNOWLEDGEMENTS

Text

The Visitor by Christine Pinsent-Johnson from *Notes Across the Aisle* (Thistledown Press Ltd., 1995). **Trombone Solo** by Stoddard King. © Stoddard King. **Foul Shot** by Edwin Hoey. Special reprint permission granted from *READ® Magazine* and published by Weekly Reader Corporation. Copyright © renewed 1989, 1962 by Weekly Reader Corporation. All Rights Reserved. **Snow Shadows** by Arthur S. Bourinot. © Arthur S. Bourinot estate. **Ride to the Hill** by Ron Taylor. © Ron Taylor. **Flood Forces Library to Close** by Beverly Ware. Reprinted by permission. Originally printed in the *Halifax Chronicle Herald*, November 1, 1996, p. A4. **9.84—Donovan Bailey Blows Away World Record** by Cam Cole. From the *Ottawa Citizen*, July 28, 1996, p. B1. Reprinted with permission of the *Edmonton Journal*. **DNA Traces Teacher's Lineage Back 9 000 Years**. From the *Winnipeg Free Press*, March 8, 1997, p. C14. Reprinted with permission. © 1997 Associated Press. **Bailey Sets Mark in 100** by Christine Brennan. From *The Washington Post*, July 28, 1996, p. D1. © 1996 *The Washington Post*. Reprinted with permission. **Perfect 10 Goes to Canadians** by Joe Concannon. From *The Boston Sunday Globe*, August 4, 1996, p. C1. Reprinted courtesy of *The Boston Globe*. **Fantastic Four Steal Show** by Doug Smith. From the *Halifax Chronicle Herald*, August 5, 1996, p. A1. **Do We Need to Use Animals in Research?** by Jane McCabe. From *Newsweek*, December 26, 1988. © Jane McCabe. Reprinted by permission of the author. **How to Buy the Perfect Bike** by Kathryn C. Kukula. From *Fitness*, October 1996. © Kathryn Kukula. Reprinted by permission of the author.

Photographs

p. 62 Robert Estall/Tony Stone Images; **p. 72** Canapress/Ed Reinke; **pp. 84-86** René Sheret/Tony Stone Images; **p. 96 (bottom left)** and **p. 99 (bottom)** Chris Carroll; **p. 96 (right)**, **p. 97-98**, **p. 99 (top)**, **p. 101** Lars Klove; **p. 106** Copyright by Electra Bicycle Company ® 1997; **p. 245** Canapress/Elise Amendola.

Illustrations

Carl Wiens: pp. 3, 4, 5, 215, 222, 223, 242 and icons; Malcolm Cullen: pp. 8, 9, 48, 97, 121, 189, 214, 219, 220, 221, 224; John Fraser: pp. 18, 22, 136, 137; Henry van der Linde: pp. 36, 37, 38, 59, 244, 251.

Cover Illustration: John Fraser